Go and Come Again

Go and Come Again

Segregation, Tolerance, and Reflection:
A Four-Generation African-American Educational Struggle

By
Jerry L. Jones, *EdD*

Professor, Emory & Henry College
Emory, Virginia

© 2011 Jerry L. Jones
All Rights Reserved.

No part of this publication may be reproduced, stored in a retrieval system, or transmitted, in any form or by any means, electronic, mechanical, photocopying, recording, or otherwise, without the written permission of the author.

First published by Dog Ear Publishing
4010 W. 86th Street, Ste H
Indianapolis, IN 46268
www.dogearpublishing.net

ISBN: 978-145750-502-7

This book is printed on acid-free paper.

Printed in the United States of America

Contents

Introduction 1

Chapter - 1: A Family Perspective 5

Chapter - 2: The Perspective of Teachers 26

Chapter - 3: Recollections of Former Students 41

Chapter - 4: Transitions of the Early 1960s 49

Chapter - 5: College Studies 66

Chapter - 6: Church Experiences 79

Chapter - 7: Work Experiences 95

Chapter - 8: Graduate and Continuing Education 108

Chapter - 9: At Home Again 118

Chapter - 10: Predicting Academic Success 137

Conclusion 151

This book is lovingly dedicated in memory of the members of my family, all four generations, who lived in the home that I have treasured and have strived to maintain. My respect for and involvement in education are a tribute to their earlier struggles.

First Generation

    Crockett S. Johnston   1844-1921

    Elmira Waugh Rollins   1840-1937

    Mary Weeks Johnston   1853-1890?

Second Generation

    Lizzie Johnston   1872-1889?

    Gillyard Johnston Waugh   1874-1945

    Wiley Waugh   1876-1933

Third Generation

    Theodore Waugh   1905-1990

    Crockett Waugh   1906-1972

    Bascom Waugh   1908-1992

    Eddie Waugh   1909-1911

    Mary Waugh Jones   1911-2005

Arthur Waugh   1913-1997

Cleopha Waugh   1915-1917

Omega Waugh   1919-1992

Fourth Generation

Robert Jones   1936-2001

The author's great-grandmother, great-grandfather, and grandmother, 1880s.
(Left to right) Mary, Crockett, and Gillyard Johnston.

The author's great-grandfather and his first grandson, 1905.
Crockett Johnston and Theodore Waugh.

The author's great-grandmother, 1920s.
Elmira Waugh Rollins.

Dr. Judson S. Hill and the faculty of Morristown College, 1880s and 1890s.

Gillyard Johnston (first row, second from left) and classmates at Morristown College.

The author's grandfather (Wiley B. Waugh) in his Glade Spring barber shop.

Introduction

FROM AN EARLY age, I realized that I wanted to be a teacher. Of course, there were so many role models who were educators—my mom, the Sunday school teacher, my elementary and high school teachers, and the many teachers who lived in the surrounding area. In later years, I have come to realize that my decision to become an educator runs deeply into my psychological makeup—the need to explain and the satisfaction derived from seeing a student succeed.

As I start to write this book, I am in the middle of my forty-first year of teaching. I started out as a high school teacher in Baltimore in 1969. In 1974, I moved back to Virginia and became a professor at J. Sargeant Reynolds Community College in Richmond. I stayed at that institution for twenty-seven years, retiring in 2001 to move back to my hometown to take care of my elderly mother. Presently, I am a professor at the highly acclaimed, nationally recognized Emory & Henry College, located only four miles from the place where I was born—the Glade Spring home that has been in my family since 1870. One could say that I had to go and come again!

Over my five decades in education—both as a student and as a teacher—I am sometimes amazed when a student appears to have a "don't-care" attitude when it comes to learning. Generally speaking, education today is accessible, affordable, and diverse. An old saying comes to mind: "You can lead a horse to the water, but you can't make him drink." From self analysis, I would not describe myself as overly scholarly. But I would describe myself as overly eager to learn. I realize that present-day youth have so many activities—so many distractions that it becomes more and more difficult to focus on academic pursuits.

Regarding public education during the Jim Crow era, the stories about my family and the stories about local black teachers and students are not overly unique, relative to the time and geographic location. In most Southern local school districts in the early years of the twentieth century, the education of Negro children was not a priority. This was a case of separate and unequal—a situation that would take decades and federal intervention to remedy.

Moving back home to Southwest Virginia has, in my opinion, given me a unique perspective about society, education, and minority status in America—past and present. The continuation of my teaching career has been rewarding. Most importantly, "coming home" has given me a unique perspective about my family, friends, church, and myself!

The author's mother, aunt, and uncle.
(Left to right) Mary, Omega, and Arthur Waugh on the front porch of Glade Spring home,
early 1920s.

CHAPTER 1:
A Family Perspective

The Johnston-Waugh-Jones Family

Formal Education, Relationships, and Relocations

LOCATED IN THE southwestern area of Virginia near the Tennessee border, Washington County borders the city of Bristol. My roots to this area can be traced back to my great-grandfather, Crockett S. Johnston. Born in slavery in 1844 from the union of a Native-American mother and a Negro father in nearby Wythe County, he settled in the Washington County town of Glade Spring shortly after the Civil War. He married Mary A. Weeks from the Abingdon area.

Commuting by train, Johnston found employment in area hotels, first at Tate Springs Hotel in East Tennessee and later at Hotel Bristol. In 1870, he built a two-story frame house that faced the railroad tracks in the heart of Glade Spring—a few yards from the depot. An analysis of the original deed indicates that he paid for the house and lot by receiving a loan from a benefactor by the name of Rush Crockett. Mr. Crockett's name appears on that original deed; a few years later, the revised deed shows his name removed. Johnston had paid the debt.

There is evidence that Johnston could read and write. What is not known is *where* and *when* he was taught—as a slave in Wythe County or as a freedman in Washington County. In my preparation for the writing of this book, I found a document in my home that was signed by Johnston in 1874. This document was a contract with the Washington County Public Schools to teach school for twenty dollars per month, payable "when funds available." This document, dated October 27, 1874, detailed various responsibilities, such as keeping the school register, seeing that the fire was made, and seeing that the floor was regularly swept. The term was for five months, and the document was prepared by C. Alderson, chairman of the school board. It is not known how long Johnston served as teacher, a job for which he was obviously minimally trained. I also found a handwritten sermon which he had authored (dated 1884) and a letter of recommendation (dated 1883) written for him!

Two daughters were born to Crockett and Mary Weeks Johnston—Lizzie in 1872 and Gillyard (my grandmother) in 1874. Lizzie Johnston died around 1889 in her teenage years, and her mother, Mary Johnston, died shortly thereafter.

There was a one-room black elementary school just beyond the Glade Spring town limits in the late 1800s (in the so-called Clarksville area). Crockett Johnston's daughters received their elementary school education in this school. As was the case throughout most of the area at the time, there was no high school training for Negro children. Montgomery County's Christiansburg Institute, founded in 1866 and located more than eighty miles from Glade Spring, was the first school in Southwest Virginia to provide secondary education for blacks—the only black high school in the entire region for decades.

Reared as a Methodist, Gillyard Johnston was sent to Morristown College in East Tennessee's Hamblen County. This two-year college was founded in 1881 by the Freedmen's Aid Society of the Methodist Episcopal Church. Supplying ministers for black Methodist congregations and teachers for black schools had been the original focus of this school. However, under the constraints of the Jim Crow South, the later mission of the school (at the time Gillyard attended) became industrial training (woodworking, brick making, and carpentry for males and sewing, cooking, and serving for females) as well as the much-needed high school training. The college was renamed Morristown Normal and Industrial College in 1901.

Born in the West Jefferson area of North Carolina in 1876, Wiley Waugh was a barber by trade; he attended Morristown College and there met Gillyard. They married in 1902. Ultimately, he set up a shop in Glade Spring's town square and cut primarily the hair of white men. He was town barber for about thirty years. Waugh's mother, Elmira Waugh Rollins, was born a slave in 1840 in North Carolina and was relocated to a neighboring Glade Spring house in the 1920s. Unlike Crockett Johnston, she had not been taught reading and writing.

As a black businessman, Wiley Waugh was able—despite the constraints of Southern culture—to provide a respectable standard of living for his family. He paid for domestic help for his wife. As children were born to Wiley and Gillyard, he added rooms to the Crockett Johnston house—the house that was, in fact, the property of his father-in-law and, subsequently, his wife. Eight children were born to Wiley and Gillyard Waugh: Theodore (1905); Crockett (1906); Bascom (1908); Eddie Howard (1909); Mary (1911—my mother); Arthur (1913); Cleopha (1915); and Omega (1919). Eddie and Cleopha died in infancy or early childhood. No birth certificates were issued for the first six children!

The Waugh children left Washington County for education and/or work; except for Mary, none returned to live in the area. In the early twentieth century (1915-1930), the education of county Negro children was not a priority. The elementary school year was for only six months, the credentials of the teachers were rarely monitored, and no black public education beyond seventh grade was provided.

Glade Spring's old black elementary school that Gillyard attended in the late 1800s desperately needed replacing by the 1920s. With the help of the Rosenwald Foundation, a new school opened in 1922. Sears president Julius Rosenwald established this foundation in 1917. This charity provided large sums of money for the construction of black Southern schools in poor, rural, and small-town areas. The local communities provided matching funds for land and labor. Wiley Waugh provided $500 toward the building's construction. This building had four rooms, including a cafeteria.

The Waugh parents took some extraordinary measures in the 1920s to educate their children beyond seventh grade. Some were homeschooled by a paid teacher, some were sent to live with cousins in Roanoke to study at that city's black Lucy Addison High School while working at Hotel Roanoke, and others were sent to Morristown College for high school training. Only the youngest child, Omega, received a high school education in Washington County. Her training came from Abingdon's short-lived black high school, Kings Mountain. Her transportation to this school was by local commuter bus; free transportation to this high school was not provided by the county at this point in time.

Struggles for education and employment were, without a doubt, a major reason the Waugh children moved to northern areas. Here is a summary of their relocations:

- After his public school education in Virginia, Theodore Waugh settled in Cincinnati, where he was employed until retirement by the C&O Railroad. He and Edna Scott Waugh were parents of two daughters—Jean and Rose.

- Crockett Waugh attended and completed his public school education in Roanoke and Washington DC. Settling in Washington, he worked as a computer technician with the Veterans Administration for more than twenty years. In his spare time, he was a caddy for golfers at the Chevy Chase Country Club, caddying for such political figures as presidents Dwight Eisenhower and John F. Kennedy.

- Bascom Waugh attended and completed his public school education in Roanoke and Baltimore. He received his bachelor of science degree from Morgan State College in Baltimore and his MD from Meharry Medical College in Nashville. Settling in New Jersey, he practiced medicine for many years in Camden. A flight surgeon and Tuskegee Airman in World War II, Dr. Waugh and his wife, Alberta Foye Waugh, were parents of a daughter, Dyann, who also became a doctor.

Commenting about her father in 2009, Dyann Waugh, a Maryland resident, stated that she admired her father as a hardworking physician "who was dedicated to the impoverished New Jersey neighborhood where his private practice was located." Additionally, she stated that Bascom Waugh rarely discussed his days as a Tuskegee Airman, often took house calls, would accept payment in the form of barter, and was a very humble person.

Bascom Waugh was the first black specialist on the Cooper Hospital medical staff and was first black president of the Camden County Heart Association. Most likely, he is the only black Glade Spring native to become a medical doctor.

- Arthur Waugh graduated from high school in Roanoke. After serving in World War II, he settled in Washington DC; there he was employed until retirement by the United States Postal Service. He was married to Mary Geneva Marshall Waugh.

- After graduating from Abingdon's Kings Mountain High School, Omega Waugh settled in Washington DC; there she was employed until retirement by the federal government—in the General Accounting Office (GAO). (As the last child born to Wiley and Gillyard, Omega was so named because of Omega being the last letter of the Greek alphabet!)

Finishing grammar school in 1928, Mary and her brother Arthur were homeschooled during the eighth grade and then were sent to Morristown College. Arthur continued his high school education in Roanoke, and Mary (staying with her brother

Theodore) continued study at East High Night School in Cincinnati. Mary Waugh married William Jones, a native of the county's town of Meadowview, in 1935. Jones spent most of his married years working in Arlington, Virginia. Mary remained in Glade Spring and raised two sons, Robert (Bobby) and Jerry (me).

The Jones marriage eventually ended in divorce in the 1940s. As I got older, I realized that there was a stigma in the local black community with respect to my mother being a divorced woman! In retrospect, however, what choice did she have? On a positive note, however, positive relationships with all members of the Jones family (especially those who lived in the Southwest Virginia area) continued through the decades, despite the divorce.

In the mid-1940s, upon the death of her mother, Gillyard, Mary returned to Cincinnati to work for about two years. Unlike her siblings, she returned to Glade Spring, raised her two sons, and earned a living as a domestic worker.

Mary Waugh Jones's life in Glade Spring was legendary. She worked in the Orr, Allison, Hutton, Williams, and Porterfield homes—among others—and in the offices of J. T. Goodman, a medical doctor. Porterfield was the founder of the world-famous Barter Theatre in Abingdon. While working in his home over a period of nearly twenty years, she met many famous people—actors, politicians, and media personalities. She had been taught piano by her mother; therefore, she served as pianist at Glade Spring's Ebenezer Methodist Church. At Ebenezer, she held numerous other positions—Sunday school teacher and superintendent, secretary-treasurer, unit leader, and trustee. With my help and the help of her brother Crockett, Mary maintained the 1870 house of her grandfather.

The Waugh children constitute the third generation of my family; their educational experiences in Washington County were minimal—not because of a lack of desire or motivation, but because of a lack of opportunities provided. Mary Waugh Jones's two sons represent the fourth generation to experience the shortcomings of Southwest Virginia's early twentieth-century standards for the public education of black children.

- Robert "Bobby" Jones, my brother, graduated in 1955 from Douglass High School in Bristol—the all-black school located some thirty miles from his home. Black students of the county began attending this school upon the closing of Abingdon's Kings Mountain High School in 1948.
- Washington County paid tuition to the city of Bristol so that black children could attend Douglass High. Students came from all sections of the county—Saltville, Glade Spring, Damascus, Emory, Meadowview, Abingdon, Fractionsville, Tumbling Creek, and Wyndale.

- The school buses provided by a private contractor were often of substandard quality—especially for the number of daily miles traveled. One such bus was nicknamed "the bread box."

- Participating in extracurricular activities was difficult—getting home from school at 5:00 p.m. and returning to Bristol as early as 6:00 or 6:30 p.m. for activities like football games.

- Bobby was offered a scholarship to attend a college in North Carolina. He had to turn it down, because our single mother could not come up with the additional funds it would have taken for him to attend. Like many of his contemporaries, he joined the armed forces (air force) after graduation. While in basic training, Bobby met a number of white enlistees who had grown up in his native Southwest Virginia area. He often commented about the disparities in the all-black and all-white high school experiences—primarily the greater variety of courses offered at the white schools.

- While serving in the air force, Bobby attended Rollins College in Winter Park, Florida.

- After his discharge from the armed services, Bobby Jones was hired as a civilian employee at Andrews Air Force Base, Bolling Air Force Base, and, finally, the Pentagon. With more than thirty-five years of government service, he retired in 1991. In 1994, he and his wife, Helen Newell Jones, relocated to Bristol, Tennessee. During this time period, he became active in the alumni association of Bristol's old Douglass High School. Bobby was stepfather to Helen's son, William, and daughter, Cheryl.

Although I was not to become six years old until November, my mother somehow managed to get me enrolled in school in the fall of 1953. This school was Glade Spring's "colored" elementary school—the same school she had attended back in the 1920s and my brother attended in the 1940s. The teacher, G. Lewis Brown of Abingdon, was the only teacher for the several grades. My recollection is that a total of twenty-five (or fewer) students were in the entire school that first year. In later years, I learned that Mr. Brown's education was from Morristown College in East Tennessee. He remained my teacher for grades one through four.

Earlier teachers at the Glade Spring "colored" elementary school included Miss Harris, Oscar Brown, C. J. Smith, Ruby Thompson, and F. L. Allen.

The school building, by modern standards, was substandard; it had a potbellied stove for heat, outdoor toilets, and a water fountain that seldom worked. There were a few books in a closet-sized library. The playground had a swing, and a basketball hoop was fastened to one side of the wooden-framed building.

Because the cafeteria was nonfunctioning, it was necessary to carry a lunch box. My lunch box, which included a thermos bottle inside, had television/movie hero Roy Rogers painted on the exterior. Sometimes my mom would wrap sandwiches in aluminum foil. I could then lay the sandwich on the stove top and heat it. A hot dog was great with such treatment! My textbooks, which had to be purchased by my mother, were carried in a large book bag.

How the teacher managed to teach the various grades is hard to imagine. There were six of us enrolled in the first grade in 1953. I recall that the older students often assisted with the younger ones.

The school was located up on a hill, about a mile from my home and just beyond the town limits. Usually, I walked with neighborhood kids to the school, sometimes using a back street. The most direct route would have been along Route 91, a main thoroughfare leading from Glade Spring to Saltville. Except for a few students living in the Plum Creek area, no students rode buses or cars to school. There were times when we were picked up by the teacher as he passed us en route to the schoolhouse; often he transported some of us home when school was out. The school was rarely closed because of inclement weather.

Small-town school days in the 1950s were before the organization of such things as Head Start, preschool, and kindergarten. I remember that interacting with other children was somewhat awkward for me, technically being an only child (my only sibling was nearly twelve years older). As a left-handed student, I was not required to write with my right hand—a situation that reportedly often occurred during the early part of the twentieth century.

Parents were involved in the school's parent-teachers association, and they met often. Year-end commencement exercises involved the entire student body. A musician/piano player, Mrs. Rosa Powell, was brought in from Abingdon to assist with the festivities. My guess is that she was paid by the teacher and/or the PTA. In retrospect, I get the feeling that funding from the county was minimal.

My mother was usually at home from work by the time I arrived from school. She was there to help me with homework—homework that was detailed and regularly administered. I must confess that my first two years of elementary school training were not overly impressive. However, by grades three and four, I started to excel somewhat.

In 1957, Mr. Brown left the Glade Spring school to take another job in Pulaski, Virginia. Our new teacher, William E. Anderson (brother of Harriet DeBose), was also from Abingdon. He was a recent graduate of North Carolina A&T State College (now North Carolina A&T State University). Because overall enrollment in the school had grown (a reflection of the baby-boomer generation), Mr. Anderson taught grades five through seven and assumed the role of principal. Another teacher, Mrs. Meredith Stuart of Glade Spring, was hired to teach grades one through four. During my three years under Mr. Anderson, my academic performance excelled. And as one of the older students, I was often called on to help with the younger ones. Perhaps it was at this point that the role of teacher began to come into my mind-set.

With very few books in the tiny library, I recall the excitement when a white resident from Bristol gave the school a set of encyclopedias. Mr. Anderson asked me to write a thank-you letter.

Mr. Anderson often gave out awards for academic performance at the end of the school year. These awards were from his personal bank account—a tribute to his dedication to the success of his students. Another end-of-school event was a picnic, usually held at an area park. No doubt, teachers and the PTA paid for many of these activities.

Another aspect of my educational maturity started in 1957—playing the piano. Although primarily self-taught, I was able to play a variety of music. I began assisting with the end-of-school festivities—including the spring music festivals that were held at one of the white schools as well as the commencement, which was held at our school. The only other time we were also allowed to go to the white schools was when immunizations were to be administered.

I also recall two spelling bees—both in competition with Abingdon's Kings Mountain Elementary. One matchup was in Abingdon; the other was in Glade Spring. Aside from displaying our academic abilities, it was interesting to meet the Abingdon students who would soon become our classmates when we all enrolled in Douglass High School in Bristol.

In the spring of 1960, we seventh graders were poised to graduate. As one feature of our graduation, we presented a play taken directly from one of our textbooks. Ironically, my role in the play was that of a "techie," spilling out computer jargon which, at the time, made absolutely no sense to me or to most in the audience. Nonetheless, the play was a big hit!

The spring of 1960 was also noteworthy because of our visit to our high school—Douglass High in Bristol, Virginia. The bus ride was agonizingly long. We made our way from Glade Spring to Emory, Meadowview, and Abingdon. The trip took more than an hour. Elementary school students from Emory were transported to their school in Meadowview.

Our bus driver, Moody Tuell, was a white gentleman who, we soon learned, was a no-nonsense, part-time preacher. "Mr. Moody" would be our bus driver for the entire five years of traveling to Douglass.

Our visiting day at Douglass High was overwhelming—meeting our future classmates as well as the many teachers— H. K. Breedlove, Steven Harris, George Dawson, Ireta Dawson, Robert Weatherton, Mildred Williams, and many others. There were so many new faces to remember and so many perceived differences in our upcoming educational transition.

Douglass School had grades one through twelve—an elementary and high school combined. One of the elementary school teachers was Georgia Polk, a Glade Spring native who sometimes rode the school bus with us.

The summer of 1960 was significant for me because it was then I took my first trips away from home for an extended period of time. The first trip was a weeklong church youth event held at Knoxville College in eastern Tennessee. This was my first exposure to a college campus. Surprisingly, I realized—even at the age of twelve—that a collegiate environment was something that I liked.

The other trip occurred when my brother Bobby purchased his first automobile—a 1956 Pontiac similar to the one that the Ricardos and Mertzes from the old *I Love Lucy* sitcom took to California. Visiting his Glade Spring home from his air force jobsite in northern Virginia, he took our mother and me to Washington DC. Once in Washington, I was amazed how segregated the neighborhoods were. There were so many black people everywhere—on street corners, in stores, and in the living areas we visited. This was so unlike my hometown of Glade Spring, Virginia.

In 1960, there were no interstate highways in most parts of Virginia. The trip took more than eight hours, following US Route 11 and other highways. The strains of the long trip were compounded because, at that period in American history in the South, black people could not stop in most places to eat and use the restrooms. I remember that Mom prepared a lunch, and we found a roadside picnic table on which to eat. Because Bobby was familiar with the route, he knew of places where restroom stops were OK. We stopped in Warrenton, Virginia; the establishment was black owned!

In Washington, we visited Uncle Arthur, Aunt Omega, Uncle Crockett, and various other former Glade Spring black residents who had relocated to the city. We also drove to New Jersey to visit Uncle Bascom and his family. Although I knew from an early age that I had an uncle who was a medical doctor, I was amazed to finally meet him and his family and to see the splendid home and neighborhood in which he lived. What a summer!

Mary Waugh (second row, fifth from left) and classmates at Cincinnati's East High Night School, 1932-1933.

William Jones, native of Meadowview, Virginia.
Mary Waugh married William Jones in 1935.

The author's uncle, Dr. Bascom S. Waugh, MD.

The author's uncle, Arthur Waugh.

Informal Education, Culture, and Enjoyment

All education does not, of course, come from school. Some see learning also as daily interactions with family and friends. For the black resident of the South, especially in the 1800s and 1900s, the church was the center of culture and social interactions. Additionally, beginning in 1915, black residents of Glade Spring had a lodge hall. Named after my great-grandfather, Crockett S. Johnston, Johnston Hall was built from materials obtained from the demolition of the original Byars-Cobb Methodist Church, the congregation of which was comprised of whites. In the early years of the twentieth century, a number of social events, including mock weddings and dances, were held in the lodge hall.

Affiliated with the Methodist Episcopal denomination, the African Union congregation was organized in Glade Spring between 1865 (the end of the Civil War) and 1873. In 1873, church trustees purchased for seventy-five dollars a one-half acre lot in order to build a church. This small church was located northeast of the then corporate limits of the town; this property adjoined a "colored" cemetery. In November of 1879, church trustees purchased a new lot for thirty-six dollars, and on it, they built a larger church. This church, centrally located and more accessible inasmuch as it was only a few yards from the town square and the railroad, was given the name Ebenezer Methodist Episcopal. It opened in May 1880, and it was located at the foot of the hill where Johnston Hall was later built. Eventually, the old church near the graveyard was torn down; the land was used to enlarge the cemetery.

Throughout the early 1900s, Ebenezer maintained a noteworthy membership for a town the size of Glade Spring. Records show that ninety-seven full-time members were listed in 1900, eighty-one in 1916, and ninety-eight in 1918. The socioeconomic conditions that caused the Waugh children and the children of other families to leave Washington County had a negative impact on the membership of Ebenezer Church. By the 1930s, church membership was listed as thirty-four.

Musical programs and special services were always an important part of the Ebenezer year. Such services provided an important bridge between local and regional churches of various denominations—Baptist, Holiness, and Methodist. The interracial or race relations programs in February were annual events for many years. As early as the 1940s, citizens of Glade Spring saw a need to improve relations between the races through church activities. In later years, such services became the rule rather than the exception.

In the 1950s and beyond, Ebenezer relied heavily on special services and letters to former members to support the work and finances of the church. At times, fundraising projects had ingenious names, such as grapefruit rally, weight rally, stay-at-home tea, silver tea, and doorknob rally. For these special services, musical visitors often came from Abingdon, Bristol, Marion, Wytheville, Chilhowie, Elizabethton, Radford, and Glade Spring.

In the absence of a fellowship hall and related facilities in the church building, use was made of the Glade Community Center in the 1950s and 1960s and Glade Spring's senior citizens' center in later years. Homecoming dinners were served in these locations as were the dinners for the Sunday school superintendents' conference, which was hosted by Ebenezer in the early 1960s. Refreshments for other special services—especially those services for which the participants traveled great distances—were also served at these locations. Without a restroom facility, church attendees often visited the home of the family directly across the street—the home of Carson and Meredith Stuart.

It is important to note that churches were segregated. Ebenezer Methodist Church, described in the paragraphs above, was *not* a part of the Holston (all white) local Methodist conference until the late 1960s. From the 1800s onward, black Methodists had their own church hierarchy—bishops, district superintendents, pastors, and staff. In our region, the black conference was named the East Tennessee Conference, and briefly, the Kentucky-Tennessee Conference. On several occasions in the early 1950s, my mother chartered a bus and took community church people and friends to the East Tennessee Annual Conference. I recall trips to the Christiansburg Institute in Christiansburg, Virginia, Morristown College in Morristown, Tennessee, and Kingsport, Tennessee.

While much is made of the separate school systems of the early twentieth century, it must not be forgotten that other institutions were also slow to deal with American racial segregation!

For entertainment, children played in backyards, vacant lots, alleyways, and streets; they rode sleighs in the winter and bikes in the summer; and they listened to radios—glorious AM radio. At night, AM radio stations located hundreds of miles away could be heard—WOWO in Fort Wayne, KDKA in Pittsburg, WLW in Cincinnati, WLAC in Nashville, and many others. During the late-night hours, WLAC played R&B music—a type of music that could not be heard on the radio stations of our area in the 1950s and early 1960s. On Sunday nights, WLAC played black gospel music. I listened to WLAC a lot while doing homework.

Notably entertaining were some of the fifteen-minute radio soap operas such as *The Right to Happiness, Backstage Wife, Young Widow Brown, Guiding Light, Stella Dallas,* and

Woman in My House. Paul Harvey News and Comment was broadcast at the noon hour, and Don McNeill's *The Breakfast Club* was presented in the morning. Nighttime dramas and comedies were equally entertaining. Among them were *Amos and Andy, Jack Benny, The Shadow, Fibber McGee and Molly, Pepper Young's Family, The FBI in Peace and War,* and *Just Plain Bill.* By listening to all of these radio broadcasts, my imagination expanded and my vocabulary increased.

Our first television set did not come until 1955. It was paid for by my brother Bobby. Before 1955, several of my mother's friends had a television—Mrs. Georgetta Pettis, Mrs. Meredith Stuart, and Mrs. Eulalia Hutcheson. It was a special treat to visit their homes and to watch TV programs such as *I Love Lucy*, and *The Ed Sullivan Show*. In those early days, only one television station could be received in our area of Southwest Virginia—WJHL Channel 11 (CBS), which was located in Johnson City, Tennessee. This station signed on the air in the fall of 1953, the same year I started in school.

Without telephones, adults visited each other—especially on Sunday afternoons. I remember my mother having extended "over-the-fence" conversations and visits with white neighbors like Mrs. Jollie, Mrs. Rhudy, Mrs. Sandefur, Mrs. Ballou, and others. During the summer months, I played with many of my white neighbors such as Richard Jollie and my black schoolmates such as the Bradley brothers, Frankie Skipper, and the Porters. My one and only birthday party was in 1950—age three. Since my birthday is November 24, I recall that it snowed heavily while my party was in progress. Margaret Porter fell in the snow!

Another fun event during the summer months was to go to the train station on Sunday evenings. Passenger trains, which went through our area numerous times each day, were our lifeline to the outside world. Even if no one was coming in or leaving on the train, going to town to "meet the train" was a major event—especially for the black community in the early 1950s. Each train was identified by a number. The eastbound train—due about 8:40 p.m.—was referred to as "Forty-Two." The adults would fellowship and the kids would play.

There were black-owned restaurants; notable in Glade Spring's early twentieth-century heydays were the restaurants of Sarah Davis, Molly Savage, and Okie Skipper Stuart. Mrs. Stuart's restaurant was unique in that it had two front entrances—one for blacks and one for whites. Neighborhoods were often mixed—blacks and whites living side by side. Schools and churches, of course, were separate. A summary of accommodations in the Jim Crow culture of early twentieth-century Southwest Virginia includes the following:

- Go to an all-black church
- Go to an all-black restaurant
- Go to the back door of a white restaurant—carry out only
- Go to the skating rink only on "colored" night
- Ride in the back of the commuter bus
- Ride in the back of other buses
- Ride in the front car (mail car) of the passenger train
- Sit in a separate waiting room in bus stations
- Sit in a separate waiting room in train stations
- Sit in the balcony of the theaters

Glade Spring winters, especially in the 1950s, were very difficult for us. The Jones house and Ebenezer Church were both very cold. Neither of these buildings had any insulation, and cracks were everywhere. Glade Spring's "colored" elementary school was not much better. Cold stoves were smelly, unpredictable, difficult to maintain, and produced uneven heat. Running out of coal during inclement weather was also problematic.

With the change to oil heat and some house repairs in the early 1960s, winter days at home were a little better. Douglass High School in Bristol was always warm, too. The bus ride to this school was not.

Even though there were several stores in the Glade Spring town square in the 1950s, it was always a special treat to go to Abingdon and Bristol for shopping. As a young child, I always enjoyed the Christmas visit to Bristol's State Street shopping district. The H. P. King department store had a toy department which was exciting. There were toy-train displays and an array of other toys. Occasionally, there was a Christmas parade during our shopping excursion. The only downside to our bus trips to Bristol was the separate waiting room for black people at the Greyhound bus station that, at the time, was located on Piedmont Street on the Virginia side of town. The room was very small, and a buzzer had to be pressed to get food service from the much larger white waiting room. Usually my mother would go across Piedmont Street and buy us carryout food at a small café that would serve black people.

Summers were always enjoyable—long days for playing outside, landscaping and mowing yards, and performing minor house maintenance jobs. It was also exciting when aunts, uncles, and my brother would come to Glade Spring for visits. Most black families would have any number of visitors, especially around July and August. I was extremely excited when a family member with an automobile came to our home and spent time with my mother and me. Initially, the only visiting family member with a car was my uncle Ted. He and his second wife, Mattie, would drive in from Cincinnati. Riding through the countryside was so enjoyable. By 1960, my brother Bobby would also visit in his automobile. He would drive in from Washington DC.

The Joneses' yard had a croquet set in the 1950s; sometimes our yard was full of players—young and old, black and white, competitive and noncompetitive. Harold Scott Taylor, who often visited from Cincinnati, was a great croquet player. A few years older than I, he was very skillful at the game!

Jigsaw puzzles were also a great pastime—especially in the days before televisions became commonplace.

Riding my bike was another joyful experience—especially during the summer. Starting to ride at about age nine, my initial bicycle trips were confined to the neighborhood—I could bike to Peery's grocery store at the end of my street and to the post office which, in the 1950s, was located in the town square. Even before my bicycle-riding days, Mom and I went to town often. Occasionally, I was allowed to walk to town alone. One memorable event occurred when I was about seven years of age. I had been sent to the Peery store to buy tomatoes. While in the store, a man drew a gun on Mr. Peery! Surprisingly, I was not unnerved. I stood my ground until the incident was resolved; my only thought was that I was not about to go back home to Mom without the tomatoes.

If my bicycle needed repair or if the tires needed air, I could go to Clyde "Bummy" Radcliff's gas station or Marvin Price's shop—both located in the neighborhood. As I got older, my bike trips took me to Plum Creek, Emory, Meadowview, and, on one occasion, Abingdon. Sometimes I rode with Frankie Skipper, Kyle Bradley, or Jimmy Bradley. Most often, however, I rode by myself. The exercise was good, the fresh air was invigorating, the transistor radio that I often had with me was entertaining, and the sense of independence was welcoming!

Despite segregation and comparative economic instability, I consider my formative years in Glade Spring to have been joyful, enriching, and appropriately structured!

The author's uncle, Crockett Waugh.

The author's uncles (left to right) Theodore and Bascom Waugh.

CHAPTER 2:

The Perspective of Teachers

MANY OUTSTANDING BLACK teachers taught in the segregated schools of Southwest Virginia in the first half of the twentieth century. This chapter profiles a select few, all of whom were born in Washington County.

Harriet Anderson DeBose

Born in Abingdon in November 1927, Harriet Anderson DeBose is the daughter of the late James R. and Louise Anderson. By growing up in this segregated area in the early twentieth century, Mrs. DeBose experienced the idea of "separate and unequal" school systems. She attended Abingdon's Kings Mountain Elementary School and Kings Mountain High School. Additionally, she attended Morristown (Tennessee) Junior College, Bluefield (Virginia) Junior College and Virginia State College (now Virginia State University) in Petersburg. Later graduate study came from the University of Virginia.

Mrs. DeBose's teaching career in Southwest Virginia was very extensive—before and after integration of the mid-1960s. In the segregation years, she taught elementary school at Big Stone Gap (in Wise County), Clinchco (in Dickenson County), Pennington Gap (in Lee County), as well as Glade Spring and Abingdon in her native Washington County. Beginning her teaching career in 1948, she noted that the segregated schools of that era were overcrowded and understaffed, teachers were underpaid, and working conditions were frightening to a newcomer. "You were on your own unless there was a caring, kind, and thoughtful teacher who was there to guide you into this new life situation."

Mrs. DeBose's first job was that of a substitute teacher, finishing out the term for a young lady who was on maternity leave. The school was located in the town of Glade Spring, about twelve miles from her Abingdon home. She traveled by bus each day. She commented, "It seemed as if those twelve miles were fifty miles. The bus stopped every five minutes to pick up or let off passengers. When you finally reached your destination, you were worn out!" The school was located at the top of a hill. There were three rooms, two outside toilets, and a space used for a "make-do" playground. Each classroom had a potbellied stove, and it was the teacher's responsibility to see that the fire was maintained throughout the day.

> I was fortunate enough to have a young man who met my bus each morning; he also performed the fire maintenance duty. In my classroom, there was a teacher's desk and chair plus four rows of desks—one for each student—a large blackboard, and a shelf to hold all the extra books. The desks were occupied by students ready to work. They had already received a good start from their former teacher. I enjoyed working with these children and had a nice relationship with their parents. The children understood me and knew I truly cared for each one of them. It didn't take long to really see they were eager to learn!

Mrs. DeBose recounted that each day at recess, the students played all kinds of games—hopscotch, ring-around-the-rosy, marble contests, baseball, and football. She sometimes joined in. "The boys were surprised to know I was really a good marble shooter, especially in the game 'pig eyes.' I won more marbles than I lost. I could also run. They weren't too pleased when I made practically all the outs in the baseball game. I wasn't picked to be on any more teams!"

When asked whether she ever faced racism when teaching at these schools—schools that were located in remote or small-town areas—Mrs. DeBose responded, "No. Where I was, it was all black, and I didn't go too far into town in either place where I lived." Pennington Gap and Clinchco schools were right in the middle of the "coalfields." She indicated that, in Clinchco, the building where she taught was a school during the week and a church on the weekends. The desks and other school things had to be removed on Friday afternoons and returned on Monday mornings. While in Pennington Gap, Mrs. DeBose roomed with a local black minister and his family. Most of the elementary school teachers were women.

Commenting on the educational quality in separate black schools, Mrs. DeBose stated, "The white students were exposed to more things—more support, more everything. [We] had limited supplies. When I was teaching at Kings Mountain Elementary, we had a supplies budget of twenty or thirty dollars per year. That wasn't nearly enough to split among the classes, so each year, the entire budget was given to a different teacher. We had no supplies whatsoever, and any supplies we needed, the teachers purchased ourselves. [But the students] seemed to have come out pretty good; students ultimately became colonels in the army, doctors, lawyers, and teachers."

Mrs. DeBose noted that black elementary school students from Damascus rode a local commuter bus to Kings Mountain School in Abingdon—a distance of about fifteen miles. They came in at 7:30 in the morning (leaving home before 7:00). The only place they had to stay was outside a local furniture store, walking up to the school when it opened. They had to remain in Abingdon until 5:30 that afternoon to catch the bus back home!

William Ernest Anderson

Born on March 19, 1932, in Abingdon, Virginia, William "Bill" Ernest Anderson was a son of James R. and Louise Anderson and a brother of Harriet Anderson DeBose. He attended Abingdon's Kings Mountain Elementary and Kings Mountain High School. In 1948, Washington County school officials decided to close Kings Mountain High School and transfer all black students of the county to Douglass High School in Bristol, Virginia. Bill Anderson graduated from Douglass High School in 1949.

Mr. Anderson received a bachelor of science degree from North Carolina A&T State College (now North Carolina A&T State University), Greensboro, in 1953. Following his graduation, he was commissioned into the United States Army as a 2nd Lt. in the 101st Airborne Division. As an army officer, he toured Fort Campbell Kentucky and Worms, Germany. His teaching career began when he substituted for his sister Harriet while she was on maternity leave from Abingdon's Kings Mountain Elementary School.

G. Lewis Brown (also from Abingdon), who had been the sole teacher at Glade Spring's "colored" elementary school throughout much of the 1950s, left the Glade Spring School in the spring of 1957 to take another job in Pulaski, Virginia. Accordingly, Mr. Anderson was hired as principal and teacher. Because overall enrollment in the school had grown, Mr. Anderson taught grades five through seven. Another teacher, Mrs. Meredith Stuart of Glade Spring, was hired to teach grades one through four.

Even though Mr. Anderson often gave out awards for academic performance and other accomplishments at the end of the school year, it took me a while to realize that these monetary awards came from his personal bank account. I was impressed by our teacher's many accomplishments at the young age of about twenty-five. He was the father of several children; he was so knowledgeable, especially about scientific and mathematical topics; he was a former officer in the army; and he drove an outstanding convertible automobile!

Another involvement of Mr. Anderson was his role as Sunday school superintendent at his Abingdon church, Charles Wesley Methodist. At this same time, my mother was the Sunday school superintendent at our Glade Spring church, Ebenezer Methodist. They worked on projects together, and they attended several superintendents' conferences in the late 1950s. I remember traveling with Mr. Anderson, my mother, and other church leaders to Pulaski, Virginia, and Gate City, Virginia, for all-day church events.

On one or more occasions while serving as our teacher, Mr. Anderson completed summer graduate study at Virginia State College in Petersburg. He took the time to mail postal cards to a number of his students, including me. Contrary to the trend of the time, *both* of my elementary school teachers were male!

Georgia B. Polk

Georgia Polk is the daughter of the late Ballard and Ardene Polk. Born in December 1929 in the Plum Creek area of Glade Spring, Ms. Polk attended Glade Spring's "colored" elementary school in the late 1930s and early 1940s and graduated from Abingdon's Kings Mountain High School in 1947. She indicated that school bus transportation was provided at this point in time from Plum Creek to Glade Spring and on to Abingdon. The Arnolds, a Glade Spring white family, had been contracted by the county to provide this transportation.

Ms. Polk attended Bluefield State College in West Virginia, graduating in 1951, with a bachelor's degree in elementary education. Later graduate study came from Temple University and Case Western Reserve University. Her master's degree was awarded by the University of Virginia.

Upon graduation from Bluefield State College, Ms. Polk began teaching in the elementary department of Bristol's Douglass School. She taught second grade during those years of segregated public education. Commenting on her teaching career in an article that appeared in the *Bristol Herald Courier* on the occasion of her retirement in 1991, she stated that she credits her mother with encouraging her to enter the education field and that she "did not regret a moment!"

As a resident of the county, but with teaching duties in city of Bristol, Ms. Polk also had the distinction of being one of only a few female bus drivers in the entire region at the time. She stated, "I was the only black female school bus driver in the county, and there were only one or two white female bus drivers then."

In the Bristol newspaper article, Georgia Polk stated: "My biggest complaint was that I didn't get enough sleep." After rising early to drive a busload of Washington County students to Douglass, she often stayed after school to await the completion of sporting and/or social events; then she would drive students back to their homes, sometimes getting back to Plum Creek as late as 1:30 a.m.

The other bus driver charged with transporting black Washington County students to Bristol's Douglass High School was a white man who was a part-time preacher—Moody Tuell. He also was a resident of the Plum Creek section of Glade Spring. Occasionally, Ms. Polk rode his bus as far as Abingdon; there her bus would be parked near the Washington County trade school. Her pickup of students began in Abingdon. This arrangement was in place for some of the years I was enrolled at Douglass. David Riddle, a Douglass student from Abingdon, was also a bus driver during this time period—driving a smaller bus to transport students living in areas like Wyndale and Fractionsville.

As a Douglass student in the early 1960s, I recall that school bus repair was handled at the county's garage in Abingdon. Oftentimes we had to sit on the bus and wait for repairs to be made. This was something I did not like, because it delayed our arrival time at home. But under the circumstances, there was no choice. There also was no choice but to have Mr. Tuell wait all day long in Bristol for the conclusion of the school day.

I recall riding the bus one night as Ms. Polk was driving us home from some after-school function at Douglass. Because the steering wheel of the bus was so soiled, she placed a handkerchief over her skirt so as not to have her clothes stained!

Ms. Polk also spoke about driving the bus in inclement weather. In the 1950s and 1960s, schools were not closed as often as today. Furthermore, there were occasions when Bristol city schools were opened even though Washington County schools were closed. Because of this situation, the buses headed to Douglass were sometimes the only school buses to be found on wintry county roads. My recollection is that Ms. Polk was a skillful bus driver!

In her very long teaching career, Georgia Polk was the recipient of an outstanding teaching award and was praised by colleagues, administrators, and students.

> My friends always say, I don't know how you have the energy. They always say, You stay busy, you stay young. The other day when I turned my letter of retirement in, [and] I kind of got wrapped up about it. These kinds of things kind of make you cry. It's like you're signing your life away.

One of the extracurricular passions of Ms. Polk's was music. Studying music under Mrs. Richardson (the wife of a local black Methodist minister), Georgia Polk soon became the primary musician at her home church, First Baptist of Plum Creek. This position she held until this church closed in 2004. My recollection is that my early piano style was much influenced by Ms. Polk, as well as Mrs. S. L. Hall (of Valley Street Baptist in Abingdon), Mrs. Elvena Johnson (of Fairview Baptist in Glade Spring), my mother, and several other church musical leaders.

Even after retirement, Ms. Polk was still quite busy as co-president of the Bristol Virginia Education Association and as a member of the Minority Advisory Admissions Committee of Virginia Highlands Community College.

Sarah Chappell

Sarah Chappell was the daughter of the late Paul E. and Mary Lou Chappell. Born in Damascus, Virginia, on April 10, 1927, she attended public school at Abingdon's Kings Mountain Elementary School and Kings Mountain High School. She attended Johnson C. Smith University in Charlotte, North Carolina, graduating with a degree in elementary education in 1948. Later she received a master's degree from Columbia University in New York.

In 1948, Ms. Chappell began teaching at Meadowview's "colored" elementary school. Originally, she taught grades one through four; the other grades were taught by Mrs. Lucille Kemp of Abingdon, who had attended Virginia State College (now Virginia State University). In later years, Ms. Chappell taught grades five through seven; Mrs. Mary Davis, daughter of Mrs. Meredith Stuart, also taught at Meadowview's "colored" school.

Ollie Hubert Cox, son of Ms. Chappell, had the distinction of having his mother as his teacher for each of his seven elementary school years. He described her as "quite the disciplinarian."

One unique feature of Meadowview's "colored" elementary school revolved around the transportation arrangement for some of its students. Students who lived in Emory (Blacksburg Community, south of US Route 11) had to remain at the school after the normal closing time until the school bus arrived from Douglass High School in Bristol. Sometimes this could be as late as 4:30 p.m. Ms. Chappell and other teachers, of course, had to remain on duty until all students had departed the building.

Ms. Sarah Chappell continued at this school throughout the segregation years, moving to an integrated school in 1965.

Meredith E. Carter Stuart

Born in Glade Spring, Virginia, on May 12, 1898, Meredith Carter Stuart was the daughter of the late Ned and Elizabeth Carter. Mrs. Stuart attended the *old* Glade Spring "colored" elementary school in the early 1900s. Commenting about her early education, she stated, "When I was a girl, the school board didn't even furnish us a crayon!" After seven years of study at this school, she traveled by train to Tuskegee, Alabama. There she enrolled in the famous Tuskegee Institute (now Tuskegee University). She studied there for five years.

Tuskegee Institute, founded in 1881, had much the same mission as Morristown College at this point in time—industrial education and farm management. At the time Mrs. Stuart attended Tuskegee, Booker T. Washington was still president of the school. Additionally, George Washington Carver, the famous botanist, was a member of the faculty. Mrs. Stuart studied under this prominent educator and made the following comment in an article that was published in the *Plow*, a local publication, in 1977:

> It was amazing what he taught us to do. For example, he could make bread and even fine cosmetics with sweet potatoes. But what I remember most was his voice. He had a voice as fine and soft as a woman.

Upon returning home to Glade Spring in 1919, Mrs. Stuart began her teaching career at a black elementary school in Saltville, Virginia.

> The school was one room, and I had to teach grades one through seven. I alternated subjects each day. I taught math, English, geography, spelling, hygiene, and science. I rode the train daily to this school, a distance of about ten miles.

In 1920 and 1921, Mrs. Stuart taught at another small school that was located in the Plum Creek area of Glade Spring—more than a mile from her home. She walked to this school each day. She told the story of once being caught in a storm en route and that a white lady who lived along the way allowed this dedicated teacher to rest on her porch.

To get an idea about the conditions found in these early schools, Mrs. Stuart presented the following summarization:

> We even had to pay for our own coal, and the building was always cold in the winter. There was a long bench by the stove where the children sat to warm their feet. Three groups of children would take turns warming their feet. But by the time they got through, the first group's feet were cold again. Water was hauled from a creek to the school in buckets. It would be hard for children today to live that way.

Mrs. Stuart also talked about the nature of school discipline in the early days. "The children then had respect for me as a teacher. Now the children are getting away with too much. Children don't have as much respect for their elders as they used to." After her marriage to Carson Stuart in 1921, Mrs. Stuart only performed substitute teaching; she and her husband raised seven children. On occasion, she taught some of her own children.

> They'd ask me, 'How are we going to call you Miss Meredith at school and Momma at home?' But they did, and I treated them just like the other children when they were in school.

After her husband's death in 1956, Mrs. Stuart went back to school. This time, she attended Virginia State College (now Virginia State University), Petersburg, during the summers. And in the fall of 1957, Mrs. Stuart returned to teaching full time at Glade Spring's "colored" elementary school. She taught grades one through four, and the principal, William Anderson, taught grades five through seven. She continued teaching at this school until segregation ended in 1965.

Mrs. Stuart, much like Ms. Polk, was a church musician. She played at Ebenezer Methodist Church, located across the street from her home. My recollection is that for a time in the 1950s, Mrs. Stuart and my mother alternated playing for the morning services. As was the case for many small-town black churches during this time period, services were held only twice a month, because preachers served more than one church. By 1958, I had joined these two ladies in Ebenezer's music department.

Not only was Mrs. Stuart a piano player, she was also a soloist. For almost two decades, the two of us visited various churches, black and white, representing Ebenezer. I was her accompanist. In addition to church performances, there were at least two occasions in the 1980s when we performed for family reunions—the Turner-Brown reunion, which was held in Bristol, and the Waugh reunion, which was held in Glade Spring. Many members of the Brown family had been students of Mrs. Stuart at Glade Spring's old Plum Creek School.

Harriet A. DeBose, Washington County native, school teacher.
Photo courtesy: Harriet A. DeBose

William E. Anderson, Washington County native, school teacher.
Photo courtesy: Harriet A. DeBose

G. Lewis Brown, Washington County native, school teacher.

Georgia Polk, Washington County native, school teacher.
Photo courtesy: Georgia Polk and Bristol Herald Courier

Sarah Chappell, Washington County native, school teacher.
Photo courtesy: Ollie H. Cox

Meredith Stuart, Washington County native, school teacher.
Photo courtesy: Jack Stuart

CHAPTER 3:

Recollections of Former Students

ONE OF THE objectives of this book is to present a multifaceted analysis of the experiences of attending schools in the era of segregation and dealing with the concurrent Jim Crow environment. With that objective in mind, I asked a select few people to detail some of their recollections of their Southwest Virginia educational and/or cultural experiences.

Elizabeth Johnson Hill attended Glade Spring's "colored" elementary school, Kings Mountain High School in Abingdon, and Douglass High School in Bristol. She indicated that some of her most enjoyable elementary school days included May Day activities, picnics in the open field, plays, and seventh-grade graduation. Her most enjoyable memories from high school were meeting other students, playing basketball, cheerleading, attending the prom, and being introduced to a variety of classes (e.g., French). The least enjoyable memories from elementary school included trying to keep warm by the potbellied stove and using the outside toilet, and her least enjoyable memory from high school was riding the cold bus. After high school, Mrs. Hill attended Swift Memorial Junior College in Rogersville, Tennessee, and she married Robert Hill Jr. Together, they raised six children, some of whom began their public school education in the county's segregated school system and transitioned to the integrated environment.

Ollie H. Cox, who lived in Abingdon, attended Meadowview's "colored" elementary school where his mother was a teacher; he also attended Douglass High School in Bristol. When asked about his most enjoyable memory from elementary school, Ollie mentioned playing in the woods during recess. His least enjoyable memory was that his mother was his teacher for grades one through seven. In high school, he enjoyed basketball, flirting with the girls, friendships, and lunch. His least enjoyable memory was that he often felt out of place. This resulted from being younger than most of his classmates. Because of this immaturity in elementary and high school, Ollie stated that he discovered that he was behind in all educational areas and that it took two years to catch up. He was able to catch up while he was an undergraduate at the historically black Johnson C. Smith University in Charlotte, North Carolina—the school his mother had also attended. He received a bachelor of arts degree in economics from this educational institution. Additional study was completed at the University of North Carolina and the University of Kansas. Ollie enjoyed an illustrative career in the corporate world and returned to Abingdon in 2001 to care for his ailing mother. He continued to live in his hometown many years after her 2005 death.

Jeanette Stuart Edmond started her public school education in Glade Spring's "colored' elementary school and graduated from Douglass High School in 1951. Like so many students in that period of time, she recalled walking in cold and inclement weather to the Glade Spring school and riding the school bus the long distance to high school—a high school experience that began at Abingdon's Kings Mountain High. Jeanette recalled that the cafeteria at our Glade Spring school was still functioning while she attended. Upon graduation from Douglass, she attended Virginia State College in Petersburg and received an associate's degree in secretarial science in 1955. Thereafter, she got a job as a secretary in the Sussex County Virginia Tech Cooperative Extension Office. She was the first black secretary there. When she talked about her early days of employment in this location, she remembered that the racial strife in this area of Virginia was unlike what she had experienced growing up in Glade Spring. However, she remained at that job for thirty-five years and was honored by the Virginia General Assembly and House of Delegates for a job well done upon the occasion of her retirement in 1990. She continues to live in the small town of Waverly, which is near her former place of employment.

Calvin Lee attended elementary school in his hometown of Saltville, Virginia. This school, which was adjacent to the all-black church of this community, was a one-room school building. One teacher taught everything for grades one through seven. This was the same school were Mrs. Meredith Stuart of Glade Spring began her teaching career back in 1919. Calvin made the following observations:

> The last three teachers of the school were Mrs. A. Johnson, Mrs. J. Martin, and Mrs. G. Easterly (Manning). Mrs. Martin was the teacher that played a large role in the students' lives in the 1950s…[a role that] had more of an impact than we realized at the time. Mrs. Martin, for example, made sure that we did our [school] work…[and also taught] us etiquette. Each year, she would have the students at her house on a Sunday morning to a formal

breakfast with complete table setting and white tablecloths...[and we] all had to be nicely dressed.

Black students from Saltville—a town which is situated in both Washington County and Smyth County—were bused to Douglass High School in Bristol. However, these students endured the longest ride of anyone attending the Bristol school; they had to travel from Saltville to Glade Spring—a thirty-minute ride—in order to catch the school bus. In the final years of this arrangement, they were transported to and from Glade Spring by one of the parents of their community.

Calvin made the astute observation that his elementary *and* high school teachers were well prepared and that they really cared about their students.

The high school teachers had to be prepared to teach two areas then, which is mostly unheard of today. The ones that stood out in my mind were Mr. and Mrs. George Dawson, Mr. Steve Harris, Mr. Robert Weatherton, Mrs. Henderson, and Mrs. Redmon. Each was unique in his or her own way.

As a high school athlete, Calvin commented about the struggles that had to be endured. For example, whenever an out-of-town game was played, county players rode two buses. One bus transported them from the game location back toward Bristol, and the second leg of the trip got the players back to Abingdon, Meadowview, Emory, and Glade Spring. Of course, Calvin still was not at home in Glade Spring. Spending the night with his grandmother—who was living in Glade at the time—was an option! Moreover, during the late summer before school began, those students from the county who wanted to participate in football had to get to practice on their own.

Calvin summarized his recollections by stating that "education was a struggle, but students did what had to be done in order to survive the times. This enabled students to become stronger adults in later years." Graduating from college in the state of Maryland, Calvin enjoyed a teaching career.

Because of the closing of the Saltville's "colored" elementary school, David Lee, a younger cousin of Calvin Lee, ended up going all the way to Bristol to become a student in the elementary department of Douglass High School. He indicated that he was not sure why Saltville school officials decided that he should be bused this great distance—a decision that may have somehow related to the fact that Saltville was then an independent school system. Nevertheless, David very vividly detailed some of the experiences of traveling such a great distance for this education—education which was coming at the young age of five or six.

> Our day started shortly after 5:00 a.m. We left the house around 6:00 a.m., well before my dad left for work in Marion. The first part of the trip started in Saltville in a local taxi that took us to the Old Glade Texaco in Glade Spring. The taxi company was Galliher's Cabs, and our driver was Bill Galliher. I guess he got paid by the Saltville school system, because they were the ones that did *not* want us in their schools. There had to be five or six of us in the taxi. I always rode in the front middle seat. One of taxis was the 'good' taxi, because it had a better heater than the other one.

The daily distance traveled was close to eighty miles—travel that often occurred during cold and inclement weather.

> The school bus picked us up at Old Glade [a junction south of the town of Glade Spring]. Because there was no interstate system then, our trip was along Route 91, Hillman Highway, and Route 11. The trip went directly through the town of Abingdon. Stoplights there caused the trip to be even longer.

David also commented about being so far from home for such a very long day. For example, if he got sick, it was necessary to remain at school until the return trip. "It wasn't the best trip when you felt good; it was even more difficult when you were sick." David attended Douglass for one year, transitioning to a Saltville elementary school when segregation ended.

Arthur Theron "Scrapper" Broady grew up in Marion, Virginia, a town located in Smyth County—the eastern county bordering Washington County. His paternal grandparents were residents of the Plum Creek area of Glade Spring. During high school years, Scrapper, his brother Jonathan, and his sister Patricia lived with their Glade Spring grandparents and attended Douglass High School in Bristol. Scrapper commented about his beginning interest in athletics while attending the segregated elementary school in his hometown—an interest which continued at Douglass; he was a member of the football team. Enrolling at Emory & Henry College in the fall of 1966 after graduating from Marion Senior High School, he became this college's first black football player.

While talking about his days at Douglass High (1961-1965), Scrapper recalled with a touch of humor about enrolling in a typing class primarily to be near his then girlfriend. Interestingly, this typing skill proved to be useful—not only in college, but also while serving in the military! One of the early black graduates of Emory & Henry (1970), Scrapper worked briefly in education and then enjoyed years of varied work experiences throughout the United States.

Jack Stuart attended Glade Spring's "colored" elementary school in the 1940s. When asked about his most enjoyable memories from this school, he mentioned Bible study on Thursdays, recess, and plays on special events. His least enjoyable memories were the whippings received for not turning in homework and staying after school for talking. There were times when his mother, Mrs. Meredith Stuart, was his substitute teacher. In Sunday school at Ebenezer Methodist Church, my mother—at one point in time—was his teacher.

Attending Douglass High School in the early 1950s, Jack mentioned that he liked working in the cafeteria, but he did not enjoy typing class, French, and book reports. Jack attended Saint Paul's College and Virginia State College. He has spent most of his adult life in Richmond, Virginia, and has come to the realization that his small-town upbringing prepared him well for living in a big city!

Earle Hutcheson is a Glade Spring native who attended Glade Spring's "colored" elementary school in the late 1940s and the early 1950s. He also attended Bristol's Douglass High School, where he was involved in football. Speaking about his high school athletic activities, Earle made the observation that protective gear worn in his football years was very limited. "We probably suffered concussions, and didn't even know it!"

Earle recalled an event of the early 1950s while attending Douglass. Getting off the school bus late one afternoon, he encountered a friend who exclaimed that Mrs. Hutcheson (Earle's mother) was going to be (or may have already been) arrested, because she refused to move to the back of the Fuller commuter bus. The story was that Glade Spring policeman Sam Blevins had been called by the bus driver because of this so-called violation of Jim Crow law. Blevins, who had been police chief for years and who had "issues" with certain black Glade Spring residents, knew Mrs. Hutcheson to be a strong-willed individual who had more knowledge about the details of these racial "issues" than many people in the town. Accordingly, the police chief did not go forward with this arrest. This Glade Spring incident occurred years before Montgomery, Alabama, resident Rosa Parks's refusal to give her bus seat to a white person!

Having served in air force, Earle and his family have lived for many years in Maryland. His brother, Richard Hutcheson, who currently lives in Michigan, also attended Glade Spring's "colored" elementary school and Douglass High School and similarly remembered the incident about their mother's refusal to move to the back of the Fuller bus. Mrs. Eulalia Hutcheson was one of the strong influences in my early childhood of the 1950s—a frequent visitor to our home and a present force and leader in Ebenezer Methodist Church.

George Fullen grew up in the small, rural Washington County community of Tumbling Creek, located north of the town of Meadowview. There was a small elementary school for black children of this community in the early 1950s, and this is where George began his schooling. Around 1953, the county decided that this one-room school should be closed and that these students should be bused to Meadowview's "colored" elementary school—an arrangement that continued until segregation ended.

When asked to comment about his most memorable public school experiences, George mentioned something about which I was unaware even though we graduated from Douglass High School in the same year. Originally, he had been in the high school class that was one year ahead of mine—the class of 1964. I remembered that he'd ended up in our 1965 class because of poor attendance and the resulting low academic performance, but I never knew why. George indicated that he was treated badly by many of his 1964 classmates and former friends—a case of being perceived as somehow different—for having a rural upbringing and a lighter skin complexion. This "outsider" mind-set caused him to travel by school bus from his Tumbling Creek home to Meadowview but to *not* get on the bus that was headed to Douglass in Bristol. He spent his days in Meadowview! To my great surprise, George reminded me that when he joined our 1965 class, there was a complete turnaround with respect to his perception of acceptance. I was so pleased to hear him say that I was one of the students who he considered to be a good friend of his. After many years of living and working in the Washington DC area, George returned to Southwest Virginia in the early 2000s and made his home in Abingdon.

Frederica Clark Cook was the salutatorian of the Douglass High School class of 1965. In the fall of that year, she enrolled as a student at Emory & Henry College. During this time period, the college's transition from an all-white student body to an integrated student body was actually just beginning. Frederica commented that she found this time of transition to be very difficult, and she stayed for only one semester. In later years, she returned to college—this time at Virginia Intermont in Bristol. She received her bachelor's degree from VI, a college located in the city in which she had lived for a number of years.

At Douglass High back in the early 1960s, Frederica was well known for her musical abilities; she regularly played for glee club performances and other events. Additionally, she was a majorette in the Douglass band. Having grown up in Abingdon, she played piano and organ at that town's Charles Wesley Methodist Church.

Carolyn Beverly Bolden attended Glade Spring's "colored" elementary school in the late 1940s and early 1950s. Her teacher during this time period was G. Lewis Brown. Because Carolyn lived next door to the school, she often went home for lunch. Like so many other former students who attended this school, she recalled many things that would categorize this school building as "far from modern." Specifically, she recalled that mice were often seen in the classroom and that, on one occasion, a mouse was discovered in her coat when she arrived at home for her lunch break! Carolyn was the valedictorian of the class of 1957 at Bristol's Douglass High School. After many years of living in California, she returned to Glade Spring in 1980 and later attended and graduated from Abingdon's Virginia Highlands Community College. When asked to comment about her positive memories about her high school experiences, she mentioned the discipline and firmness of the teachers—a caring that is sometimes lacking in modern-day education. She enjoyed her high school coursework; it prepared her well for further study and for the workforce.

Margaret Preston Davis also attended Glade Spring's "colored" elementary school and Douglass High School. She graduated from Douglass in 1956. When asked to comment about her memories of growing up in Glade Spring during the time of segregation and the Jim Crow culture, she detailed an experience that is still vivid in her mind. Margaret and a white friend were traveling in the car of the friend's mother—a trip that was taking them to Saltville. The two youngsters went into a gas station to sit down and have a Coca-Cola. The gas station attendant, of course, shook his head—an indication that a black person was not allowed to be seated in the establishment. The white friend, after inquiring as to the nature of the problem, became very agitated and exclaimed that her family would *not* be giving business to this station in the future. Ironically, Mrs. Preston (Margaret's mother) chastised her daughter for "doing something that she knew was wrong." After many years of living in northern areas, Margaret Davis returned to live in Glade Spring more than a decade ago.

Because of a family relocation, Charles Jones attended Abingdon's Kings Mountain Elementary, as well as Bristol's Douglass Elementary. When asked to comment about the differences between the two schools, he indicated that the academics were essentially the same. Recollections of differences had more to do with the different cultures—Abingdon being a much smaller community than Bristol. However, Charles did mention that at

Douglass Elementary, there was usually one teacher per grade; at Kings Mountain, one teacher may have taught two grade levels. Regarding the environment of the Jim Crow South of the 1950s and 1960s, Charles recalled that his parents, grandparents, and other black community leaders were very specific about telling black children to always do what white people requested—a reflection of the time and geographic location, something that could easily present internal conflicts when one became an adult in the world at large (such as in the military). Charles returned to the area in 2007.

Nina Porter Doak is the only surviving person who attended all twelve years of public education with me—Glade Spring's "colored" elementary school from 1953 to 1960 and Douglass High School from 1960 to 1965. Many of our recollections about our Southwest Virginia education are the same—walking to elementary school in all kinds of weather and withstanding the long ride to Douglass for five years. Moreover, Nina and I also share something else in common—attending Ebenezer United Methodist Church and singing in the choir. When Nina moved to Nashville, Tennessee, more than forty years ago, she ended up joining a Methodist church there that reminded her of the little church back home.

CHAPTER 4:

Transitions of the Early 1960s

WITH THE COMING of the spring season in 1960, a number of transitions began. The seventh-graders of Glade Spring's "colored" elementary school (Leona Hayes, Nina Porter, Margaret Porter, Paul Ervin, Kyle Bradley, and Jerry) were fast approaching the day when we would graduate and start our journey into secondary education.

As one feature of our graduation, we presented a play taken directly from one of our textbooks. Although I cannot remember the title of the play, I do recall that my assigned role had something to do with computers. Of course, in 1960 computers were not commonplace in society. The play, however, was a success. Kyle Bradley's performance was outstanding; he played the role of a father figure—gray hair, pipe, and everything!

Commencement exercises required a lot of practice—marching, speaking, and singing. There was also the fun of our annual school picnic, which was held at a local park that admitted black people. Even with all of these fun things, there was some apprehension about going to high school. Our high school, of course, would be some distance away—Douglass High in Bristol. The distance traveled daily was significant—about thirty miles one way. But at age twelve or thirteen, some of us considered such traveling an adventure, especially if we were members of a family without an automobile.

We visited our new school in May. The bus ride was long—winding our way from Glade Spring to Emory, Meadowview, and Abingdon into Bristol (Route 91, Route 11, Hillman Highway, and other roads). The trip took more than an hour. Elementary school students from Emory were transported to their school in Meadowview. All of us who lived in downtown Glade Spring walked to the depot in the town square to wait for the bus. The bus came at 7:30 in the morning and we did not get home until 5:00 p.m.

I received a number of gifts for my elementary school graduation. Some of the gifts were money, including silver dollars. Many of these silver dollars I still have. I used some of the money I received as graduation presents to buy my first transistor radio. This radio was purchased from the Spiegel catalog of Chicago. Even though this radio was AM only, it was very powerful; it pulled in, with the help of an exterior antenna, distant stations—from Virginia, North Carolina, and Tennessee. I enjoyed attaching it to my bicycle basket and riding through the countryside. During the summer months, I also enjoyed yard work, wallpapering, painting, and mowing the yards of others such as Mrs. Allison (my mother's employer), Mrs. Rhudy (neighbor), and Mrs. Meredith Stuart (church member).

The summer of 1960 was also significant for me because of two trips taken. As a member of the Ebenezer Methodist Church Sunday school, I was selected to attend a weeklong youth conference. This conference was held on the campus of Knoxville College, then an all-black college in eastern Tennessee. In previous years, this conference was held at Morristown College. It was changed to the Knoxville school because of construction work on the Morristown College campus.

Reverend Leroy Coffey, the Ebenezer Methodist Church pastor, drove classmate Nina Porter, Sunday school officials, and me to this event on a Sunday afternoon. As I recall, this youth gathering consisted of religion classes and games; it concluded with a worship service. All participants stayed in college dormitories and ate in the college cafeteria. At the end of the week, we returned home on the Greyhound bus from Knoxville to Bristol and a Fuller bus from Bristol to Glade Spring. In 1960, blacks were still sitting in the back of the bus. Nina and I each had to make a presentation before the assembled Sunday school attendees. We returned to a similar youth gathering in 1962, this time at Morristown College. Our return trip this time was via a Trailways bus from Morristown to Abingdon and a Greyhound bus from Abingdon to Glade Spring Junction. We had to call for a taxi to get into the town of Glade Spring. We were still sitting in the rear of all of these buses!

The second trip in 1960 for me was to Washington DC. This was a family trip. My brother, who was ending his term in the air force, purchased his first car; it was a 1956 Pontiac. Even though he was not living with our mother and me, it was such a change to know that someone close to me actually owned an automobile! This trip to Washington occurred after school closed for the summer. In 1960, the Interstate Highway System was not available in most of the United States and there were no interstate highways in our area of Virginia. Therefore, the trip to Washington took more than eight hours. Much of the journey was along US Routes 11, 250, and 29, through just about every Virginia town imaginable—Chilhowie, Marion, Christiansburg, Wytheville, Radford, Roanoke, Charlottesville, Warrenton, Culpeper, and many others! At this point in American Southern history, black people could not stop in most places to eat and use the restrooms. Mother packed a lunch, and we ate on a roadside picnic table. Our restroom stop was at a black restaurant in Warrenton!

When we arrived in Washington DC, there was an element of culture shock for me. The city was so segregated! There were black people everywhere—on street corners and in all of the neighborhoods we visited. This was so unlike the small towns of Southwest Virginia.

In 1960, all of my mother's siblings (except two who died in childhood) were still living. Omega, Arthur, and Crockett were all in Washington. On a Sunday morning, we drove to Haddonfield, New Jersey, and visited Uncle Bascom, his wife Alberta, and their daughter Dyann. Uncle Bascom *barbecued* steaks *outside*. An outside barbecue was something I had never seen before!

The Bascom Waugh home, located in a primarily white neighborhood, was very elegant. The story is told that when their house was being built in the early 1950s, Alberta (Aunt Bert) would dress up like a maid whenever she visited the construction site of her new home. This was done so as not to alert the neighbors of the upcoming move of blacks into the neighborhood. Integrated neighborhoods were not commonplace then, even in northern locations.

Mother and I returned to Glade Spring by train. Sometime during the summer of 1960, Uncle Crockett agreed to pay for renovations to our house—the 1870 house built by my great-grandfather, Crockett S. Johnston. After Wiley Waugh, my grandfather, died in 1933, house repairs were rarely done. The foundation was unstable, and the upstairs porch was about to fall down. These repairs were desperately needed.

The eighth grade class at Douglass High School in the fall of 1960 had slightly over thirty students—from Washington County and the city of Bristol. We were divided into two homeroom sections. One section was assigned to Mr. George Dawson, who was the industrial arts teacher, and my section was assigned to Ms. Barbara Johnson, the business teacher.

English, mathematics, geography, and science were the cornerstones of my study for the eighth grade. Additional courses included glee club and public school music. I found these two courses to be very helpful in that they added much-need theory to my God-given music abilities. Membership in the school band was reserved primarily for Bristol students, because elementary school preparation and after-school practice were not possible for county students.

Class	Teacher
English	Mildred Williams
Geography	Mary Redmon
Glee Club	Mildred Williams
Mathematics	Ireta Dawson
Music	Mildred Williams
Science	Robert Weatherton

The academic performance of our eighth grade class was amazing. A record number of us were on the honor roll, attaining an average of 3.00 (or higher) on the 4.00 scale. My recollection is that some of these honor students included Katie Sue Trent, Frederica Clark, Leona Hayes, Nina Porter, Betty Cooley, Mary Clark, Sylvia Cochran, Kenneth Carter, and several others (more than 30 percent of the class). I was also on this list. In retrospect, I believe that I became too obsessed about maintaining a high grade point average. My adolescent rationalization was that college would not be possible without an academic scholarship. I had no athletic ability!

The fall of 1960 was also noteworthy locally because of a murder in the Glade Spring area. Two or more members of a white family by the name of Graham died; police tear gas set the house on fire. Our school bus driver, a part-time preacher, had been called to the scene to talk with the perpetrator. On the way to school the next morning, Mr. Moody was so shaken that he missed one of the turns in our route!

In November, the presidential election of 1960 was so close that when we arrived at Douglass School the day after the election, we still were not sure if the new president would be Richard Nixon or John F. Kennedy.

During the winter of 1960-1961, I suffered with an episode of strep throat and missed three days from school; Dr. J. T. Goodman came to the house to see me. At the time, my mother was cleaning his office, and I vividly remember him warming his hands over the coal stove in our living room and telling her that she did not owe him for the visit! I ended up having the tonsils removed in the summer of 1961 at Johnston Memorial Hospital in Abingdon.

Three days missed from school in the eighth grade and three days missed in the eleventh grade were my only absences in five years of going to Douglass. I had three years of perfect attendance—ninth grade, tenth grade, and twelfth grade. Many of my schoolmates had similar attendance records. Even with the distance traveled daily, we were reluctant to miss school. The school bus ride was such a waste of time—more than two hours a day for five years. And during the winter, the ride was extremely unpleasant. The bus was cold unless you sat behind the driver near the heater. By the time I got to Bristol, my feet would be so cold that I could hardly walk. My mother's remedy was to heat a brick on the stove, wrap it in foil and cloth, and give to me to carry to school. This remedy worked!

By 1960, nearly everyone in our community had a television. And the news of racial unrest, political upheaval, and violence was shockingly constant. For example, as high school students during the Cuban Missile Crisis in 1962, many felt that the calmness of the 1950s—the *Leave-it-to-Beaver* era—was over. I remember that one day in the fall of 1962 we had a civil defense drill and were dismissed from school early. The joke on our school bus was that if there were a Soviet attack on the United States, everyone would be in their shelters at home and we would still be on the school bus somewhere en route from Bristol to the county!

There was the assassination of civil rights leader Medgar Evers in the summer of 1963 and the bombing of Birmingham's Sixteenth Street Baptist Church in the fall of 1963. Even though these events were quite a distance away, many of us realized that Virginia was also dealing with the issue of racial segregation. It was astonishing to realize that in Prince Edward County *all* public schools were closed from 1959 to 1964 rather than integrate. What was the world coming to!

The ultimate shocker, of course, came on Friday, November 22, 1963—the assassination of President John Kennedy in Dallas, Texas. Many of us were in fifth period glee club when Principal Breedlove announced over the intercom that the president had been shot. By the time we got to sixth period (Typing II), his death had been confirmed. The bus ride home was one of the *longest* and *quietest* of our entire five years of attending Douglass High School. Of course, by Sunday, the presumed assassin, Lee Harvey Oswald, was also dead—his killing captured on television. This happened on my sixteenth birthday. The consensus among so many of us Douglass students was that uncertainty would be continually commonplace. Another headline was the Vietnam War. With each passing day, the scope and the seriousness of this conflict became increasingly evident to most of us.

Despite the turbulence of the early 1960s, there were many joys for us during our five years at Douglass High School. For me, one of those joys was participating in the glee club. There were trips to music festivals in Greeneville and Kingsport in Tennessee as well as Gretna and Fieldale in Virginia. Under the expert direction of Mrs. Williams and with classmate Frederica Clark serving as accompanist, we also sang at white schools and black churches in the immediate Bristol area. One of our signature songs was Wilhousky's arrangement of the "Battle Hymn of the Republic." The joy of a standing ovation from a racially diverse Bristol audience was astoundingly rewarding. I have never experienced anything like it since!

Because of her illness on one particular occasion, the glee club performed without Mrs. Williams. I can remember sitting at the piano to sound the chord that started an "a cappella" selection. Other favorite songs of mine were "The Heavens are Telling," and "The Lord Bless You and Keep You."

When the new addition to Douglass High School was dedicated in the fall of 1963, I was asked—as a representative of the student council—to make a speech of appreciation to the assembled audience of faculty, students, parents, city politicians, and school officials. I memorized the speech that I had personally authored, and I was caught off guard by the praise received for the delivery of it.

In the spring of 1964, I was asked by my mathematics teacher, Joseph Means, to apply for admission to a math institute that was to be held during the upcoming summer on the campus of Emory & Henry College. This institute was sponsored by the National Science Foundation. Each day en route to our all-black high school in Bristol, we passed by the entrance to this college. I knew that this was a highly acclaimed school that, at this point in time, was minimally integrated, if at all. In fact, most schools in Southwest Virginia in 1964 were not integrated. Nevertheless, I applied and was accepted.

The math institute ran from mid-June to mid-July. It consisted of about twenty-five high school students from around Virginia as well as five local high school math teachers. The coordinator of the institute was Dr. Thomas Graybeal, and the teachers were Dr. Ray Hancock and Professor Ruth Biggers, members of the college's math faculty. I represented Douglass, the black high school in Bristol, Virginia, and Flora Penn represented Slater, the black high school in Bristol, Tennessee. I stayed in Hillman Hall, a boys' dormitory, and Flora stayed in one of the girls' dormitories. Even though it was summertime and the campus was not full, there was the sense that the two of us were participating in more than just a math institute; we were "integration pioneers."

On one occasion, Dr. Leidig, dean of the faculty, called me into his office. He stated that there was a rumor on campus that I was being mistreated in the dormitory. Of course, there was no basis to this rumor, but the query did catch me by surprise. My recollection is that all of us got along very well; we lived together, ate together, studied together, and went to class and study sessions together, and there was a lot of time for socializing.

The Emory & Henry summer institute also consisted of two field trips—one to Virginia Tech, about ninety miles from the Emory campus, and the other to the University of North Carolina (Chapel Hill), about 150 miles from the Emory campus. Dr. Graybeal called me into his office to outline travel details. Because of the length of these two trips, he felt that rest stops would be in order. Therefore, he called the Holiday Inn in Wytheville to see if there would be a "problem"—stopping there with a group that had two black students included. He informed me that this Wythe County business agreed there would not be a problem! At UNC, we visited a planetarium, and at Virginia Tech, we saw—among other things—a mainframe computer. Of course, all of these locations were a first for me.

It is an overstatement to say that my performance at the Emory & Henry NSF Math Institute was outstanding; it was mediocre, at best. My overall ranking was about fifteenth out of the twenty-five student enrollees (tenth in homework and twentieth on the final exam). The only topic I remember was binary arithmetic—something that would "come again" when I started my study of computers! Nevertheless, the institute was a life-changing event—my first interracial academic experience.

Driver's education is a common feature of high school. At Douglass, this was difficult because of our scheduling—six periods of study with no time after school (catching the bus back to the county). In 1964, however, it was decided that driver's education would be offered on Saturdays. I rode the local commuter bus (Fuller bus) to Bristol and completed this training with Mr. Dawson. A family friend, Elsie Preston, took me to Saltville so that I could take my test and get my learner's permit.

Limited funds and no automobile made getting to the prom difficult. For my junior year, I went by taxi, and for my senior year, Elsie let me borrow her car.

In the 1960s, the Tri-Cities television stations had locally produced programming—gospel and country music, game shows, and shows relating to community interests. One such weekly program on Bristol's WCYB-Channel 5 was *Classroom Quiz*—a high school game show that could be compared to today's *Jeopardy* or to Allen Ludden's *College Bowl* of an earlier time. As president of the Douglass Student Council in the fall of 1964, I made the suggestion that Douglass High School should participate in this television program. Even though the show had been on the air for a number of years, no black school had ever participated.

We decided to have a mock quiz in order to select participants. Eventually, the three probable contestants were chosen—Peggy Newton from Emory, Rocky Clay from Bristol, and me. We were booked to appear on the television program at the last minute when another school canceled. Our appearance was scheduled in December, near Christmas. My plan was to get to Bristol by train; however, at the last minute, I discovered that the train was going to be delayed. What to do? Again, Elsie Preston came to the rescue. She drove me to the television station just in time!

Although we did not win (the "wheel" was against us!), we presented a good showing. I answered one question presented to me, and to this day, I don't know how I came up with the answer (divine intervention, no doubt): *"Who was the last wife of comedian Ernie Kovacs?"* The correct answer was "Edie Adams." At the beginning of the show, it was my pleasure to present a brief, memorized introductory speech about our school. After our appearance, no other black school ever appeared on the show!

On several occasions, I had to get to Bristol for various activities related to school. For example, there were the guest disc-jockey appearances on WFHG radio on several Saturday afternoons. WFHG-AM was a leading rock-and-roll radio station during this period in time. Even though the available number of records by black artists was minimal, we did our best to pick the songs that the Douglass students wanted. I can recall catching a ride to WFHG; after the broadcast, I walked about a mile from the station on Valley Drive to Lee Highway to catch the Fuller bus back home. When I became the president of the student council, I had to attend beginning school year events with the faculty. Since the Fuller bus did not run at night, traveling to and from Bristol was then more challenging. Sometimes I called on Ms. Georgia Polk of Glade Spring, Reverend Leroy Coffey of Bristol, and even the Greyhound bus for transportation. By 1964-1965, I no longer had to sit in the back of buses.

Being a member of the Douglass High School Student Council was also rewarding even though the experience probably did not lay the groundwork for my entry into Glade Spring town politics some forty years later. Aside from arranging the Douglass appearance on *Classroom Quiz*, the most noteworthy events relating to student government were our trips to state conferences. I remember two such trips—Portsmouth and Lynchburg in Virginia. Principal Breedlove and Coach Harris drove several of us for these trips. Although I don't recall much of the discussions that occurred during these meetings, I enjoyed the traveling, staying in a motel for the first time, and interacting with fellow Douglass students like David Riddle and Scrapper Broady. Students from the hosting schools were equally entertaining. Additionally, I was astonished about the size of these schools (I. C. Norcum in Portsmouth and Dunbar in Lynchburg) in relation to Douglass.

Whenever we traveled eastward into Virginia, the black populations were notably larger. Therefore, all of the schools were larger. In some ways, we felt like we were "Tennessee cousins" rather than actual Virginia residents. Nevertheless, the trips were rewarding. Perhaps at this point in time, I realized that traveling eastward would be my course of action after my Douglass school years had ended. Usually the eastward trips included a rest stop at the Greyhound bus station in Wytheville, one place that was OK with a black group stopping to use the facilities!

Another television phenomenon for our area during this period in time was the editorial segment on the evening local newscast of WCYB television. This segment was produced and delivered by Walter Crockett, the station's news and public affairs director. Over a period spanning several decades, he talked about a variety of topics. We were astonished, however, when, in the early 1960s, his chosen topic was about the ridiculous arrangement of black high school students in Washington County being bused all the way to Bristol, Virginia—a situation that had been in place since 1948.

Although not involved in sports, I managed to attend just about every football and basketball game. Douglass played other black high schools from the region—Douglass of Kingsport, Artie Lee from Dante, Langston from Johnson City, George Clem from Greeneville, and Douglass from Elizabethton. The biggest rival, of course, was Slater from Bristol, Tennessee. When football games were played in the Bristol stadium, they had to be held on Thursday nights since Friday nights were reserved for the white schools. Because we got back to the county so late on Thursday nights, this meant that Friday school days came much too soon! On one occasion, our football game was held in the stadium of the all-white John S. Battle High School, located in the Washington County suburbs near Bristol. The opposing team was Bland High School. I recall that, back in the 1950s, some of the Douglass games were held in Saltville, Glade Spring, and Abingdon, and the school's homecoming parades were routed beyond Bristol into the county as far as Abingdon. Moreover, during this earlier time period, Douglass students were occasionally bused to Glade Spring to skate at the roller rink on "colored" night. The rink was located directly behind my house! By the 1960s, the skating rink had closed, and with the one exception of the one football game at John Battle High, no Douglass games were played anywhere in Washington County and no Douglass parade was seen outside Bristol.

Under the expert direction of Roland Seward, the only white member of the Douglass faculty, the band was another very popular extracurricular activity, primarily available to Bristol residents. (As mentioned earlier, after-school practice and elementary school preparation would have been difficult for residents of the county!) Not only did the band participate in Bristol events like the televised Southeastern Band Festival in the fall, it also traveled to Abingdon for the Tobacco Festival Parade and to Chilhowie for the Apple Festival Parade. Additionally, the band participated in regional music festivals that were held during the early spring at one of the black schools. Douglass's marching band was famous for its R&B beat!

In the spring of 1965, the Washington County School superintendant, E. B. Stanley, unexpectedly appeared on our school bus just as we were about to depart from Douglass High. He abruptly announced that new federal funding guidelines would no longer permit the county to send students to the Bristol school any longer and that, in the fall of 1965, black students would attend the county high school nearest to their homes. We were in shock! One of my senior classmates wanted a clarification that we would be allowed to finish out the current year at Douglass. In later years, I often wondered how my life would have been different if my senior year of high school had been at the predominately-white Patrick Henry High School, located about three miles from home!

Because of the announcement that segregation of Washington County schools was soon to end, the Douglass High School class of 1965 immediately assumed a unique title—the last graduating class of the school. Listed below are the members of that class:

Anderson, Ronald S.	Abingdon
Austin, Carolyn L.	Meadowview
Black, Arthur D.	Bristol
Bradley, Kyle V.	Glade Spring
Brown, William M.	Bristol
Carter, Kenneth W.	Bristol
Carter, Mary E.	Meadowview
Carter, William H.	Meadowview
**Clark, Frederica	Abingdon
Clark, Mary E.	Abingdon
Cochran, Sylvia A.	Bristol

Coleman, Hilda L. — Abingdon
Cooley, Betty V. — Abingdon
Cox, Ollie H. — Abingdon
Duff, William H, Jr. — Bristol
English, Theresa L. — Bristol
Foote, George F. — Bristol
Foster, Nancy J. — Wyndale
Fullen, George C. W. — Tumbling Creek
Fulp, Victor E. — Bristol
Fuqua, Joseph L. — Fractionsville
Hayes, Leona V. — Glade Spring

Jones, David L. — Fractionsville
*Jones, Jerry L. — Glade Spring
Lee, Calvin C. — Saltville
Logan, Erkward, Jr. — Meadowview
Lowe, Robert B., Jr. — Abingdon
Porter, Nina I. — Glade Spring
Rawley, Barbara F. — Bristol
Ross, Rollen A. — Bristol
Trent, Katie S. — Abingdon
Washington, James C. — Bristol
Watkins, Isaac W. — Meadowview

*First Honor
**Second Honor

When the members of the class of 1965 went across the stage during commencement exercises, we, of course, shook the hand of Principal Breedlove. We also shook the hand of Dr. Joseph B. Van Pelt, superintendent of Bristol schools, and Dr. E. B. Stanley, superintendent of Washington County schools. Interestingly, today both of these men have local schools named for them.

Under the expert direction of faculty class advisors George Dawson and Ethel W. Rogers, another memorable closing ceremony for the class of 1965 was Class Night. It was at this event that awards were presented to outstanding members of our class. Three churches—John Wesley Methodist of Bristol, Lee Street Baptist of Bristol, and Ebenezer Methodist of Glade Spring—presented gifts to church members who were also members of the class. Listed below are some of the other awards presented:

- Cameo Club Most Deserving Student Award
- Club Unique Cooperation Award
- DAR Citizenship Award
- DAR History Award
- English Essay Award
- Highest Average Award
- Industrial Management's Most Improved Senior Award
- Kiwanis Club Outstanding Girl Award
- Lions Club Outstanding Boy Award
- Raytheon Science Award
- Rescue Mission Most Religious Student Award
- Rotary Club Mathematics Award
- Student Council Award
- Tri-Cities Circle Club Award
- Virginia Parrish Study Club Award in English

It was my great honor to receive nine awards. Most of these awards came from the various civic groups that recognized my scholastic performance. However, the Ebenezer

Methodist Church Award was uniquely special. Presented by Mrs. Annie Bradley Vannoy, these awards—presented to Nina Porter, Kyle Bradley, and me—were a tribute to our many years of church service and of studying, singing, and performing gospel music throughout the Tri-Cities area.

One of the Douglass Elementary School teachers, Miss Alice Mapp, was presented an award during our Class Night ceremony. She had been a teacher for decades! Because of this special presentation, a WCYB-TV news team suddenly appeared in our Douglass auditorium. In addition to reporting on Miss Mapp's award, the team also reported on our class awards. We got back to the county just in time to hear legendary TV-5 newscaster Merrill Moore mention our names on the eleven o'clock television newscast!

Because the Douglass High School gymnasium/auditorium was not adequate for commencement, this graduation event was held at Virginia Junior High School (now known as Virginia Middle School). Uncle Crockett and Uncle Arthur traveled by train to attend my graduation. Mrs. Porterfield, Mother's employer, loaned us her car so that we could drive to Bristol to attend the activities!

Earlier in my senior year, I had some difficult choices to make with regard to my future education. Having grown up in a family that was unfamiliar with collegiate opportunities and choices, I was not sure of my course of action. Because of my study at Emory & Henry College during the summer of 1964, some of the officials at that college felt that it would be good if I enrolled there. Dr. Graybeal, director of the 1964 Summer Math Institute, actually visited my Glade Spring home and talked with my mother and me. As Douglass High School senior valedictorian, there was also the opportunity—because of a scholarship—to attend the all-black Virginia State College in Petersburg. My mother allowed me to make the decision about which college I would attend. Uncle Crockett thought I should be a "pioneer" and go to Emory & Henry or another "white" school. Realizing that college work—especially the freshman year—would be a challenge, it was my personal belief that going to Emory and assuming the role of "pioneer black in a predominately white school" would be too much pressure. Additionally, I believed that my involvement in local church music might be a distraction and that being so close to home might not be the best for my overall maturity. Therefore, I choose Virginia State—a school which, as late as the 1940s, was named Virginia State College *for Negroes*!

Douglass High School, Bristol, Virginia.

The author doing high school work.

Methodist Church Summer Youth Institute, Morristown College, 1962.
Nina Porter (last row, second from left) and the author (third row, seventh from left).

National Science Foundation Math Institute, Emory & Henry College, summer, 1964. Flora Penn (first row, seventh from left) and the author (first row, first from left).

CHAPTER 5:
College Studies

DURING MY SENIOR year at Douglass High School, the idea that I would be the first in my immediate family to attend college started to feel like a reality. There were no community colleges in Virginia in 1965, and most four-year, historically white colleges, including Emory & Henry, were minimally integrated—if at all. With a background of twelve years of all-black public school education, my strong belief was that I should attend a predominantly black college. Additionally, my high school, because of its size and nature, did not have advanced-placement or honors courses; my collegiate preparation was uncertain.

The only all-black public college in Virginia in 1965 was Virginia State College (Petersburg) with its Norfolk division—a division that eventually became Norfolk State. Even though there were a few all-black private colleges in Virginia then (Hampton Institute, Virginia Union, and St. Paul's, for example), my financial profile was such that Virginia State provided the best viable option. The yearly cost of attending Virginia State then was about $900. As the valedictorian of my high school graduating class, I would receive a state tuition scholarship of $200 for each of my four years of study. It was up to me to *find* the remaining $700. I researched a number of grants and loans to help fund my education: a national defense student loan, an economic opportunity grant, and a Virginia teachers loan. Negotiating all of the paperwork was very daunting. I had to get character references from my mother's employers and had to get documents notarized at our local bank. But by summer, my financial profile seemed to be secure.

Located in the eastern region of the Old Dominion, Virginia State College was nearly three hundred miles from my home. I had not been to Petersburg and had not even seen pictures of this educational institution. Given the distance and given our financial situation, making a preliminary trip to visit the school did not seem likely. I would see this college for the first time in September!

Passenger trains were still running in most parts of Virginia in 1965. Those were the days before Amtrak. All that I would need to do to go to college was to walk to the train depot in the Glade Spring town square. Friends and family mentioned that I would have to change trains in Roanoke. All of these details were overwhelming!

It is correct to say that I was nervous about leaving home for college. I am not sure what my mother really thought about it. Outwardly, her quiet reassurance—the belief that everything would be OK—gave me solace. Essentially, she would be alone for the first time in her life—living in the Glade Spring home in which she and her siblings were born and reared. Many church members and other citizens in my hometown gave me words of encouragement and expressed their prayerful support. Similar words of encouragement were heard upon my graduation from high school earlier in the year.

The fall semester at Virginia State College began in September. I was scheduled to leave Glade Spring on train number 42, departing about 8:40 p.m. Of course, my mother was the only one to go with me to the train. I felt anxious and nervous, but excited and hopeful.

As mentioned earlier, the change from the Southern Railway system occurred in Roanoke—this line extended northward on to Washington and beyond. The Norfolk and Western line went eastward through Southside and, ultimately, on to Tidewater. My arrival in Petersburg was at about 5:00 the next morning. A few other students onboard were heading to Virginia State. We waited until daylight to get a taxi to the school—a school located on a hill above the Appomattox River.

Founded in 1882, Virginia State College was established as a result of the Morrill Act—legislation that required a state to either open land-grant colleges to all races or to establish a separate school for blacks. Rather than integrate the all-white, existing Virginia Tech, the Commonwealth of Virginia created this all-black school—the first of its type (a fully state-supported, four-year collegiate institution) in the United States. This school has had the following names:

> Virginia State Normal and Collegiate Institute
>
> Virginia State Normal and Industrial Institute
>
> Virginia State College for Negroes
>
> Virginia State College
>
> Virginia State University

On the wall of the Petersburg train depot, there was a map of the city. This map listed the college as "Virginia State College for Negroes." I thought this to be unusual, because I had never heard of this school referred to in this manner—a manner which, in today's world, would be considered politically incorrect. Even though the phrase "for Negroes" was removed from the college's name in 1946, the map in the train depot in 1965 still reflected this segregation-era title!

The transition to college life was challenging. Few students at Virginia State came from my region of the state. Many of the kids from Central, Southside, Tidewater, and Northern Virginia had never heard of Bristol or other localities near the Tennessee and Kentucky borders.

It was in Petersburg that I first learned that I had a "southern" accent. During my freshman year, there were a few instances of name calling—the perception that I was not "hip" enough and a little bit too country. It also did not help that I was skinny, talked differently, and did not have that urban stride to my walk. I walked more like Barney Fife than George Jefferson. Fortunately, these issues subsided by the start of my sophomore year. Whenever I hear issues relating to bullying in present-day America, I am reminded of those early days at Virginia State. Being different was—and still is—difficult. Some things seem to never change!

Because I had done well in all of my high school courses, there was not an overriding sense of what my college major would be. For my first semester at Virginia State College, mathematics was my declared major. After that first semester, I decided to switch to business education; high school courses like bookkeeping and typewriting had been some of my favorites. Interestingly enough, my first semester of college was not very impressive—mathematics and chemistry courses proved to be difficult. However, my study habits were solid. In both elementary and high school, my studying was extensive, organized, and productive. By contrast, I am sometimes shocked when I hear many of my current college students (even those with high GPAs) comment that their high school studying was minimal or nonexistent!

Any male student enrolled in a four-year degree program at VSC, a land-grant school, was required to take ROTC (Reserve Officers' Training Corps)—military science. This training, a two-year requirement, consisted of such things as drilling and ceremony, military history, military protocol and courtesy, civil service exam preparation, map reading, rifle marksmanship, and leadership. There was also a merit-demerit program in place. On Wednesdays, cadets were required to wear army uniforms all day and to practice on the drill field from 3:00 to 5:00 p.m. Additionally, cadets were permitted to wear army uniforms when traveling home for holidays and were awarded travel discounts. A discounted round-trip train ticket between Glade Spring and Petersburg was thirteen dollars! When I got off the train for my first Thanksgiving holiday, one longtime friend questioned whether I was in college or in the army!

Initially, I did not like ROTC. Even though I did surprisingly well on the firing range, I sometimes felt like Gomer Pyle on the drill field. Nevertheless, I persevered. Using my office and business skills, I spent a lot of time in the offices of the ROTC headquarters, earning merits. Fifty merits earned in a semester would raise a final average by one letter grade. I ended up having an average of A for three semesters and an average of B+ for one semester. At the end of the two-year military science basic training, I was asked to consider enrolling in the advanced program—a program that would have me becoming a commissioned army officer upon graduation in 1969. I declined this invitation largely because I did not see myself ready for military service. When I finished my two years of ROTC training in 1967, the college made military science strictly voluntary. Many colleges in the United States made this decision in the late 1960s in response to Vietnam War opposition.

Members of the faculty at Virginia State College were very impressive to me. Many had terminal degrees from major northern universities. Most were black. However, during my time at VSC, a number of white professors were hired. I had white teachers for English, history, military science, and philosophy.

At the start of the second semester in January 1966, I began my studies as a business education major. The head of this department was the legendary Ella F. Mundon. Professor Mundon had been at the college for decades and was described by many as being tough in the classroom. I found her to be engaging, with a well-developed sense of humor, and she reminded me of the strong black women in my family and in my hometown. Other notable black teachers in the School of Commerce during the late 1960s included Singleton, Long, Duke, Ritchie, Turner, Blount, Harris, Mason, Hayes, Hunter, Brickhouse, Jemison, McDaniel, and Whitlow. Although many of these faculty members did not have doctoral degrees, their teaching skills, in my opinion, were quite superior. They were all excellent role models.

By my sophomore year, much of my coursework was in the business area—accounting, finance, stenography, and typewriting; my GPA had improved significantly. (I was on the dean's list for one semester.) For each semester of the sophomore year, I was enrolled in nineteen semester credits, a total that included the two-credit military science. This course load was exhausting; however, I was determined to graduate on time, without the necessity of summer study.

The general education requirements at Virginia State were very comprehensive—philosophy, music, art, communication skills, literature, sociology, speech, physical education, psychology, and other courses. Additionally, there was an English proficiency exam that had to be passed. Overall, I did well in all of these areas. One of my strongest areas was writing!

The teacher education program was smoothly run. There was a self-kept student record of progress which I still have today, more than forty years after the fact. There were classroom observations and public school visits as a part of this program's requirements.

By the end of my junior year, I was consistently on the dean's list. After a less-than-average freshman year punctuated with occasional verbal harassment, I had managed to become a respected member of the VSC upper-class hierarchy. I even performed work-study duties for Professor Brickhouse, a member of the accounting faculty. During my junior year, I had a roommate, Robert Dock, from Salem. He had knowledge of and interest in Southwest Virginia—Bristol and other localities near the Tennessee border. He was a business administration major. Therefore, we were enrolled in some of the same courses, such as business law. Occasionally, on the large VSC campus, I ran into Francis Thomas Riddle, Sylvia Cochran, Willie Hopkins, and Mary Ann Brown—Douglass schoolmates who were from Bristol. They were attending VSC during this time period. At one point, Sylvia and I were enrolled in the same course—philosophy.

Virginia State College was not immune to the student unrest that was sweeping across the United States in the 1960s and early 1970s. I recall that there were protests and class boycotts relating to such things as the cafeteria and other campus services; there were political protests relating to the Vietnam War and other issues. During this time, my personal agenda—to finish college on schedule—did not allow for much involvement in protests and/or boycotts! When it came to studying, I discovered that I could spend hours and hours in my room; I needed few breaks. All I had was an AM/FM radio that my brother had given me for Christmas in 1966. Interestingly enough, this radio's FM band picked up the audio signal from one of the television stations in Richmond—WTVR Channel 6 (CBS). I made this accidental discovery one Saturday night. Turning the dial, I heard something that sounded like *The Jackie Gleason Show*. Sure enough, Channel 6 was being received! This station became my frequent study companion.

As mentioned earlier, I felt it important to not be attending VSC for summer sessions; there were no finances to do so. Moreover, I looked forward to the cooler climate and familiar surroundings of Southwest Virginia. To help my finances, I tried to find summer work in the Glade Spring area—work in addition to my routine maintenance of my mother's home and yard, Ebenezer Church, and Dr. J. T. Goodman's offices. Jobs were hard to find in my hometown area—especially for a few summer weeks. But in the summer of 1966, I was hired by the Olin Mathieson Chemical Corporation to work at its Saltville plant. This company had a policy in place that allowed the hiring of students during the summer. The duration of my work experience was only for six weeks; however, the pay was very good. I worked in the caustic acid department, helping to move and load barrels. Although a few black men worked at the plant, I was the only black working in my department. Everyone treated me well. My only problem was getting to work. My work schedule varied. There were three shifts. Sometimes I could ride the Fuller bus; often I was given a ride by various Glade Spring white men who worked at this Saltville workplace—John Sandefur, Ralph Routh, Ballard Bise, and others. On more than one occasion, I spent the night (from 11:00 p.m. to 7:00 a.m.) in the guardhouse and caught one of the early morning buses back to Glade Spring!

In the summer of 1967, I was hired again by the Olin Mathieson Chemical Corporation—this time for the entire summer. The pay this time was even better—so much so that I managed to buy my first car. This car was a 1960 Ford Falcon, which I bought for about $295. Owning an automobile, even an old vehicle, was a life-changing event for my mother and for me! Often I would drive my car to the Glade Spring custard stand, which was located at the intersection of Route 91 and Fleet Road. There I would meet Kyle Fogleman, who lived in the Plum Creek area. I would ride with him to work in Saltville. He and I worked together, drilling for *salt* on a high hill overlooking the town! We became good friends, and in later years, I visited him and his wife in their home. During the 1967 Saltville work experience, a high school classmate, Calvin Lee (a Saltville native), was also employed in the salt/well-field department. He was a college student in Maryland.

Overall, these summer work experiences were very rewarding. The regular workers, almost all white, were very accepting! Unfortunately, the student employment program at the Saltville plant was not available for the summer of 1968. The only job I could find for that year was that of a dishwasher at a Bristol-area restaurant. Additionally, Uncle Crockett paid me to paint our Glade Spring home.

One of the highlights of my junior year at Virginia State College occurred during the spring of 1968. Professor Turner, our business law professor, asked me to attend a state meeting of Phi Beta Lambda—the Future Business Leaders of America. The meeting was to be held at a hotel in Richmond in early April. Professor Turner, in consultation with Professor Mundon, believed that I should enter the "Mr. Future Business Teacher" contest. This event occurred on the weekend following Dr. Martin Luther King's assassination.

The keynote speaker at this conference was a young state legislator named J. Sargeant Reynolds. Reynolds later became lieutenant governor, but he died in office in 1971 at the age of thirty-four as the result of an inoperable brain tumor. The Richmond-area community college was named for Reynolds, and I ended up teaching at that school for twenty-seven years, starting there in 1974! At this point in time, few male students were enrolled in business education degree programs across the state of Virginia. Therefore, only three of us entered the "Mr. Future Business Teacher" contest—one black student from Norfolk State College, one white student from Virginia Commonwealth University, and I entered from Virginia State College. Even though I was often shy around strangers, I felt comfortable in the contest interview. I recall that one of the questions dealt with my thoughts about how computers would change the nature of business education. I won the contest!

In the fall of 1968, I decided to take my car to Virginia State. I had never driven a long distance before. My brother felt that driving on the several highways in such an old vehicle was not a good idea. However, knowing that in a few months I would probably have to drive to a student-teacher location, I felt it was important to get long-distance traveling experience then rather than later! My mother, who had never learned to drive, decided to go with me and give moral support. The highway trip was long, but uneventful. After riding with me all the way to Petersburg (a distance of almost three hundred miles), Mom quickly got on a train and rode back to Glade Spring—arriving in our hometown around midnight. Our neighbors, Mrs. Okie Stuart and Mrs. Rhudy, were standing on their front porches with their lights on to see that Mom made it down the street to her house OK. Decades after this event, I still get tearful thinking about how blessed I was to have such a supportive mother, family, neighbors, and friends! For my hometown, the term "close-knit" was *then* so appropriate.

As a recently inducted member of Pi Omega Pi, the national business-education honor society, I was asked by Professor Mundon to attend the annual meeting, held during the 1968 Christmas break at Chicago's Palmer House Hotel. Traveling by train to Chicago, another VSC student from the Richmond area joined me in Cincinnati. When we got to the train station in Chicago, we tried to hail a taxi. We were continually passed by. A bystander informed us that we were not being picked up because we were black and that the drivers assumed that we wanted to go to an all-black neighborhood. The bystander intervened and helped us get a taxi. In retrospect, I wonder if we should have been holding a sign that said "Palmer House."

The return trip from Chicago was made difficult by a snowstorm; all of the trains were cancelled or delayed. Our alternative was to return to Virginia by bus. Our bus eventually broke down, delays occurred, and my return to Glade Spring necessitated my walking from the interstate to my home—a distance of about two miles at 3:00 on a cold December morning.

Except for Pi Omega Pi, my involvement in social and extracurricular activities at VSC was nonexistent. In retrospect, I suspect that some of the reasons for my nonparticipation included the sense of feeling different as a result of my first-year "outsider" experiences, the need to study almost all the time to compensate for a less-than-average academic performance in my first semester, and/or elements of my personality that I did not fully understand. Nevertheless, there were frequent informal discussions in dorm rooms, as well as before and after various classes. However, there were no formal memberships on my part—no fraternities, no clubs, and no romantic interests!

The business education major at VSC was, essentially, a hybrid major consisting of business administration and accounting courses, general secondary education courses, office and clerical courses, and business teacher methodology courses.

- Accounting—four semesters
- Economics—two semesters
- Business law—two semesters
- Typewriting—three semesters
- Stenography—two semesters
- Office management
- Clerical practice
- Office machines
- Business principles
- Business finance
- Business English
- Data processing
- Foundations of instruction
- Audio-visual instruction
- School health education

Methods of testing in business education

Methods of teaching business education

My student-teaching experience at VSC was coordinated by the Secondary Education and Business Education departments. There was a rule that stated that a student could not be sent to the high school from which he or she had graduated. This certainly was not a problem for me—my high school, which no longer existed, would have been three hundred miles away. Originally, Professor Mundon planned to send me to a predominantly black high school in Richmond. But at the last minute, she changed my assignment to T. C. Williams High School in Alexandria, Virginia—a relatively new school at the time. I was pleased with my student-teacher location, near some of my relatives in Washington DC.

My teaching assignment began in January 1969; arrangements had been made for me to live in a lady's home that was located near the school. I decided to drive my old car from Glade Spring to Alexandria, even though urban driving was something that was beyond my comfort zone!

I was scheduled to teach general business, business mathematics, and accounting—grades nine, eleven, and twelve. The school was very large, and the student body and faculty were racially diverse. I was well received by everyone at the school, had no problems relating to both black and white students, and was highly rated by the onsite supervising teacher and my faculty supervisors from VSC. I returned to Petersburg in March to finish out the second half of this final semester.

Commencement exercises for Virginia State College were scheduled for June 1, 1969. Required to return to the college a day or two before graduation activities, I decided to ride the Greyhound bus rather than drive my aging vehicle. My mother's plan was to go by train to Washington and join my brother, aunt, and uncles—traveling to Petersburg by automobile. Because the commencement was on Memorial Day weekend, traffic—according to my brother, the driver—was problematic. However, they all (Aunt Omega, Uncle Crockett, Uncle Arthur, Bobby, and Mom) made it to the festivities on time. Of course, this was a momentous event for my family and for me. Surprisingly, I was the only business-education major to graduate with honors.

Mom almost missed her train in Washington, and I almost missed my bus in Petersburg. Nevertheless, we both made it safely back to Glade Spring. With the start of summer, I made plans to get started on graduate study at East Tennessee State University in Johnson City—hoping that a few graduate credits would give an added boost to my job-seeking pursuits.

The author studying at Virginia State College, 1967.

The author in Virginia State College ROTC uniform, 1967.

Pi Omega Pi, Business Education Honor Society National Meeting, Chicago, 1968. Virginia State College Professor Ella F. Mundon (fifth row, fifteenth from left) and the author (third row, tenth from left).

The author's graduation, Virginia State College, 1969.

CHAPTER 6:

Church Experiences

Learning to Play Piano for Church

AS MENTIONED IN earlier chapters, my mother often struggled financially—especially in the early 1950s. I can recall that there were times when she was making thirty-five or fifty cents per hour, cooking and cleaning in the homes of several prominent white Glade Spring families. For a while, we were on welfare, and at one point shortly after my birth, Mom sold her mother's piano just to make ends meet.

As a youngster in the early 1950s, I was always fascinated by music—listening to the radio and often singing along with the many songs of the pre-rock-and-roll era—the McGuire Sisters, Patty Page, Perry Como, and countless others. I even remember having a toy piano that had about ten keys. I loved to bang on it! I tried, although unsuccessfully, to replicate the songs that I had heard in church.

My foray into the art of piano playing increased in the mid-1950s when the pastor at Ebenezer Methodist Church was Leroy Coffey. Reverend Coffey owned an old automobile (a Nash, I believe) and often drove members to various other churches, as well as to homes of black citizens in and around the Glade Spring area. On occasion, after morning church services, a few church members—including my mother and me—would be transported by Reverend Coffey to the Plum Creek area to have dinner with an elderly lady by the name of Maggie Brown. Miss Maggie was also a distant cousin of my mother. After dinner, the adults would go into the parlor to talk, and I went into the hallway where Miss Maggie's piano was located. I played, usually with one finger, the songs just sung in church! In retrospect, I am amazed that I was allowed to "play" her piano, even though it was a rather old model.

Following my brother's graduation from high school and subsequent entry into the air force in 1955, Mother's financial situation improved slightly. Accordingly, when Miss Maggie made plans to move to Florida in 1957, Mom decided to buy her piano. The purchase was made for about sixty dollars, paid in several installments. Apparently, Mom had sensed that I had some musical potential, and she made a way for this talent to be explored. Even though I knew that Mom often played for church, I did not know then that my grandmother, Gillyard Waugh, had also played (she died in 1945, before I was born).

So in the fall of 1957, the large, upright piano was delivered in a pickup truck to our home. The truck belonged to a white neighbor by the name of Lawrence Thomas. Six or seven strong men helped with the transport of the piano on a Friday evening. It was decided that this musical instrument would be placed in the dining room (against an interior wall), next to the chimney. The piano came with a round, adjustable piano stool. The excitement that I felt was unimaginable!

My mother and I found an advertisement for a "starter kit" on piano instruction in a magazine; she purchased this kit for less than three dollars. The kit came from the Dean Ross Piano Studios in New York. The kit consisted of a cardboard, color-coded cutout that was placed to the left of middle C. This cutout guided me in the formation of a few three-key major chords. A rectangular paper sheet was placed to the right of middle C; this sheet labeled the keys. After some practice, I was able to construct several chords with the left hand and play the melody of a few songs included in the kit with one finger of the right hand. By Christmas of 1957, I was able to play "Silent Night" in C major. During Sunday school, I played this Christmas carol. This was my first public musical performance!

By early spring of 1958, I was able—with some guidance from my mother—to play a few hymns. One of these hymns was "Pass Me Not O Gentle Savior." My mother and Mrs. Annie Bradley, a church member, decided that it would be nice if three of her sons (Kyle, James, and David) and I would learn to sing this hymn, which I was playing with "gospel flair." (This gospel flair I had obviously picked up from some of our visits to other churches in the region—Fairview, Plum Creek, or Valley Street *Baptist*.) We practiced this song often and prepared to make our debut at a Mother's Day special afternoon service in 1958. We were named the "Four Ds." (Need we guess what *D* stood for?) Many in the audience were shocked. Few people in the area knew that I could play, and few knew that the four of us could sing or do anything other than be "little *devils*." Later that year, church members decided that our singing group should be expanded. This was the start of the Ebenezer Methodist Church Junior Choir.

In the spring of 1958, Uncle Crockett came for his annual visit to his old Glade Spring home place. He lived most of his adult life in Washington DC. After a talk with my mother, he agreed to purchase the piano lessons that followed the starter kit that I had been using for several months. The cost was less than $50. Given Mom's financial circumstances at the time, "real" piano lessons would not have been an option. I remember Uncle Crockett saying that piano playing was not something boys did when he was growing up in the early 1900s, but he felt that "times had changed." In retrospect, I am amazed that I wanted to develop this potential musical ability. There certainly were no male piano players that I witnessed in my hometown!

Even though we were very young, by 1960, the junior choir provided most of the music for morning services at our church—Ebenezer Methodist in Glade Spring. The membership of this choir included Kyle, James, and David Bradley; Nina, Margaret, and Violet Porter; and Paul Montgomery. I played the piano. Not only did we perform for morning services at our church (second and fourth Sundays), we performed at other churches for afternoon programs. Reverend Coffey was famous for taking us to churches out of town—Rogersville, Tennessee; Norton, Virginia; Pulaski, Virginia; Bristol, Virginia; Rural Retreat, Virginia; and other places. Sometimes the Stuart sisters (Linda, Wilma, and Phyllis) joined us, even though they regularly attended Fairview Baptist Church.

Gospel music, at this point in time, was rarely heard in Methodist churches—even black Methodist churches. However, our church elders supported us in singing this version of music that we loved so much. At a church in Wythe County, we actually got a lady to shout! We were not sure what was going on, because this was something we had not experienced before.

Gospel music, even in the 1950s and 1960s, had a beat much like R&B music. As young black kids, we were instinctively drawn to this music. Even though our life experiences were limited, we still could identify with many of the lyrics of our songs. Often Reverend Coffey would exclaim excitedly, "Sing, children, sing!"

From a variety of television shows (local, syndicated, and network), we picked up many gospel music styles—southern gospel (white quartettes, primarily) and, occasionally, black gospel—Clara Ward and Mahalia Jackson (often showcased on variety programs like *The Ed Sullivan Show*). There were several local black church choirs and musicians that we emulated. One such choir was the Valley Street Baptist Church Choir from Abingdon. Under the expert direction of Mrs. S. L. Hall, the wife of that church's minister, this choir's musical performances were ultimate examples of great black gospel music of the

1950s and early 1960s. Mrs. Hall's piano style was very inspiring to me. Whenever she and her group visited our Glade Spring church, I made a point of sitting in the front row so that I could watch her play!

Gradually, my piano playing improved. My chord structures expanded, my "swing bass" was perfected, and I was able to figure out what the right hand should do to augment the melody. In essence, I was learning to play by ear, despite the training that I gleaned from the mail-order music lessons. As a child and adolescent, I never really thought about this musical ability being a gift from God. Today, I know better!

As mentioned in an earlier chapter, I attended weeklong church youth conferences during the summer of 1960 and the summer of 1962. The first conference was at Knoxville College, and the second conference was at Morristown College. Both events had a talent night, so I decided to play the piano. These events were my first and second times playing a baby grand piano. (I would not play another baby grand piano for about fifteen years!)

Favorite songs of the Ebenezer Junior Choir included "Jesus Lifted Me," "Where Could I Go," "We are Soldiers," "Ride on King Jesus," "The Old Ship of Zion," "Until I Found the Lord, "Lilly of the Valley," and "Jesus Be a Fence." Another signature song for us was a song that we heard on television, performed by the white southern gospel group known as the Happy Goodman Family. The song was entitled "Give Up and Let Jesus Take Over." What a joy it was to sing this upbeat, happy, and inspiring selection! Initially, we were the only area group to perform this song. And when another group finally copied us, we felt that in some way we were recognized as musical talents far beyond our years!

On one occasion, the Ebenezer Methodist Church Junior Choir was asked to put on an entire concert at a small church in Emory, Virginia—Mt. Zion Baptist. Nina Porter and I got together and wrote a narrative about each song. We did our research by scanning songbooks, sheet music, and album covers. She read these introductions before each song. This performance was probably our most noteworthy presentation. Interestingly enough, the year of this performance was 1965; it was in that year that Nina, Kyle, and I graduated from Douglass High School. As was the case for so many young black people before us, we left the area. Younger members of the choir also eventually left. Our singing experience, fine while it lasted, had come to an end! A year or two later (during the summer), I was asked to return to Mt. Zion Baptist Church to play for my first wedding. Wedding music, different from hymns and gospel songs, presented a challenge for me. But after much practice, I was able to function well!

There was another Glade Spring group for which I sometimes played—The Melodyetts. This all-female group was managed by Elsie Preston. There was also an all-male group that I sometimes played for; this group was managed by Robert Hill Jr.

Ebenezer Church Survival

Ebenezer Methodist Church, built in 1880 on the "other side of the tracks" in Glade Spring, had its beginning because of the segregation of churches in the area. The all-white Methodist Conference was called Holston, and the all-black Methodist Conference was called East Tennessee (and briefly, Kentucky-Tennessee). Socioeconomic circumstances in Southwest Virginia in the early twentieth century had an effect on the black population of the region. Because of few jobs and the absence of high school education, this population group diminished dramatically. Accordingly, the membership at Ebenezer was very small when I was a child in the 1950s. I can remember that on many Sunday mornings, the attendance was usually less than ten, and most were women. These ladies, all of whom had low-paying jobs or fixed incomes, struggled to keep the church going.

At various times during the year, especially during warm-weather months, special fundraising programs were held. These programs were usually musical services presented on Sunday afternoons. Letters were often sent to former members who had moved to large cities, such as Columbus, Dayton, Washington, New York, Cincinnati, Knoxville, and Roanoke. These former members were asked for financial support. The proceeds derived from these services produced enough funds to keep the church going for another year.

Ebenezer Methodist Church was a frame building erected just a few years after the end of the Civil War. Although repairs were often needed, this was difficult to do because of limited funds. A percentage of money raised had to be sent away to the Methodist Conference for benevolences. Through most of the 1950s, the church was heated by a potbellied stove that was located in the middle of the sanctuary. The stovepipe was suspended with wires across the ceiling to the chimney on the eastern wall. During one Sunday school session in the 1950s, the stovepipe actually fell—no injuries and no damage done, however!

When Reverend Leroy Coffey was pastor (1954-1965), occasional repairs were done. Reverend Coffey had a lot of connections in the white communities around Bristol where he lived; he worked in the Greyhound bus station in Bristol, Virginia. He was able to find contractors who were willing to come to Glade Spring and work on the church. He was also able to find low-cost building materials—materials that were often discounted because of imperfections. Therefore, during the Coffey years, much-needed repairs were completed including new windows, a new floor, and a used "warm morning" coal stove (the suspended stovepipe was removed!).

Even after Washington County public schools were integrated in 1965, young black people continued to leave the region. Once an individual moved away, rarely did that individual return. When I was in college (1965-1969), I always spent summers in Glade Spring. Although I had very little or no income at this point in time, I tried to maintain the church. Many times, this was a matter of doing some small, much-needed repair. For example, I replaced one or two windows that had fallen out.

Beginning in the 1960s, Ebenezer preachers were full-time ministers at a much larger black church in Abingdon. This church was named Charles Wesley Methodist. There were several noteworthy pastors during this time period. One such pastor was the Reverend M. C. Hickman. He would come to our Glade Spring church on the second and fourth Sundays at about 12:30 p.m.—following his 11:00 a.m. services in Abingdon. One particular Sunday in 1968 sticks out vividly in my mind. When Reverend Hickman arrived, we could tell that he was visibly upset. During his sermon, he detailed an experience that had happened earlier that day. The incident occurred at Abingdon's Johnston Memorial Hospital. The reverend went to this hospital often, visiting and praying with the sick. Somehow he encountered a very, very sick white lady, and he asked if he could pray with her. Her response was, "*I don't want no nigger praying over me!*" Again, this was 1968!

The all-white Holston Conference and the all-black East Tennessee Conference merged in 1968. For the next thirty years, however, the pastors at Ebenezer were black. Church membership did not increase. Essentially, there were no black youth left in the Glade Spring neighborhood in which the church was located. Still the church struggled onward. When I finished college in 1969, I at least had some income. As a public school teacher, however, this income was comparatively low. Occasionally, I tried to have church repairs done, and there were grants and donations from other churches and conference sources.

The Church in Southern Culture

During the late 1970s, the Reverend William Weldon preached at Ebenezer and Charles Wesley. Pastor Weldon and Mrs. Weldon (who later also became a minister), were very energetic additions to the Washington County black community. During

Pastor Weldon's tenure, Charles Wesley Church was able to sponsor an event that featured the Reverend Martin Luther King *Sr.* as the keynote speaker. This event was held in the chapel at Emory & Henry College. If I remember correctly, the date for this service was the summer of either 1978 or 1979—about a decade after the assassination of Martin Luther King *Jr.* Because I was spending the summer with my mother in Glade Spring (away from Richmond where I was a professor at a college there), one of my Abingdon cousins, Ann Newton, then a member of the Charles Wesley Church Choir, asked me to play piano music as people gathered for the service (this was my third time playing a baby grand piano!). When the choir came in, I took my seat in the audience, and I ended up sitting next to WCYB-TV Channel 5 newsman Johnny Wood, who had been assigned to cover the event. Wood and I noticed something unusual when Reverend King entered the pulpit—he was accompanied by an *armed* Virginia State Police trooper. It seems as though a threat against "Daddy King" had been received. Again, this was the late 1970s!

As mentioned earlier, the Methodist churches integrated in 1968. The hierarchy of the Holston Conference of the United Methodist Church often asked the members of Ebenezer to close their small church and merge with the all-white Byars-Cobb Church in Glade Spring. Ebenezer members, including my mother, were not very excited about this proposed merger. Although relations with Byars-Cobb had always been comparatively good, the Ebenezer members were sensitive about the legacy of their church, which was such a pivotal force in the local black community for many years.

In the late 1800s, members of Ebenezer sold a parcel of land to repair the church. In retrospect, this probably was not the best decision to be made inasmuch as the church was left with only the land on which the edifice stood. No more than two or three feet separated the church and fence on all sides. Some adjoining white property owners were very supportive of the church; others were not. One property owner strategically planted trees along the property boundary and subsequently allowed these large trees to dangerously drape over the edifice; an owner also maintained a pigpen against the church. Another owner would always operate his lawn mower during Sunday morning services and tied his continually-barking dog against the structure. At one point, a rental property was used by college fraternity members who decided to have a bonfire dangerously close to the wooden-frame, historic church building.

The street in front of Ebenezer Church was one of the last streets in the town of Glade Spring to be paved. It was a dusty, gravelly mess well into the 1960s. Even though this street was heavily traveled and was *not* a dead-end route, the maintenance and upgrades of some streets were often perceived to be dictated by the racial and/or socioeconomic demographics of a neighborhood. There was one incident in the 1950s when an article appeared in a local newspaper indicating that our church was going to be moved back several feet so that this street could be widened. This proposed move had never been discussed with the church membership! Fortunately, the project never happened. Even as late as the year 2000, a major construction venture in front of the church was initiated by the town without any input from church members!

During some of the later years when my mother and her contemporaries were running the church (I was still living in Richmond at the time), certain repair projects were initiated. One in particular could have been tragic. A local contractor was paid to rewire the church. Later examination revealed that this person had left most of the 1920-era haphazard wiring in service above the sanctuary ceiling. A longtime friend of mine, Jim Bradley, discovered this potentially dangerous problem after the ceiling lights suddenly stopped working. With the help of one of his friends, he corrected this problem and charged a nominal fee of $100.

The seating capacity of Ebenezer is roughly 100-120—large enough for most church services. However, for certain events, more space and easier accessibility were required. Therefore, several funerals for Ebenezer members were held at the nearby all-white Grace Presbyterian Church. The funeral of Wiley Waugh, my grandfather, was held at this church in the 1930s, Carson Stuart's funeral was held there in the 1950s, Charles Seals's funeral was held there in the 1960s, and Meredith Stuart's funeral was held there in the 1990s. Over the years, relationships among Glade Spring churches—black, white, and denominationally diverse—have been good.

Over a period of more than seventy years, my mother had several responsibilities at Ebenezer Church. One of those responsibilities was Sunday school teacher. In the early years, her students were the young people. As this population group declined, her focus became the older children and adults. She was the ultimate role model as far as multitasking was concerned—making the fire, cleaning the church, playing the piano, preparing the communion, teaching Sunday school, serving as Sunday school superintendent, planning the summertime picnics, purchasing and/or preparing Christmas treats, preparing church paperwork, planning trips to East Tennessee Methodist Annual Conferences, and inviting pastors to our home for Sunday afternoon dinner! In later years, she served on committees that promoted area-wide "preaching missions" that featured nationally-known preachers and musicians. These events were often held in the auditorium of Patrick Henry High School. One of these interdenominational events featured a former astronaut as keynote speaker.

For my last two years of living in Richmond (1999-2001), I was coming home about two weekends per month. These trips were necessitated because of my mother's declining health. Additionally, the academic year of 1998-1999 was a sabbatical year that was also spent in Glade Spring. A benefit of this hometown living was that I was able to do more for Ebenezer Church. In 1998, the Holston Conference sent us our first white preacher—Laura Blair, a senior at Emory & Henry College. Laura, an Abingdon native, was *not* our first female preacher, however. The first was Sally Crenshaw from Tennessee, serving back in the 1930s.

During the summer of 2000 when John Roe of Bristol was serving as pastor at Ebenezer, I was able to organize a special service celebrating the 120th anniversary of the church. Reverend Mrs. Greta Weldon (the wife of former Ebenezer pastor William Weldon) was invited to be guest speaker. Dinner was served at Glade Spring's senior citizens' center, located not far from the church. The anniversary celebration was profiled in *Washington County News* (WCN) in Abingdon. WCN reporter Carol Fields interviewed many of the church members and attended one of our morning services. The celebration was also profiled by WCYB television in Bristol. A reporter interviewed me in the church and compiled a "Faith Focus" feature that was aired on several newscasts. All of this publicity was helpful to the church and marked a turning point in my rededication to the survival of this historic place of worship.

Before leaving Richmond for good, I met several times with Glade Spring native Jack Stuart and his wife, Angie. The Stuarts owned the property across the street from Ebenezer (the former Stuart family home). Because there was no parking space available at Ebenezer (not even roadside parking after the new curbing was constructed by the town of Glade Spring), I discussed with the Stuarts the possibility of donating their property to the church. Landscaping of this property was paid for with funds received from the estate of my brother, Bobby Jones. The parking lot project was completed in 2002!

When my position at Emory & Henry was upgraded from adjunct professor to visiting professor in 2002, my income was such that I was able—over a period of time—to finance additional improvements to Ebenezer Church. Some of these improvements included a new piano, exterior vinyl siding, interior paneling and insulation, carpeting, air conditioners, new windows, pew cushions, structural underpinning, and electrical wiring. Over a period of four or five years, more than $25,000 was spent—artwork and a sound system were donated by my friends the Tollivers of Emory, and other United Methodist churches donated paraments. (Incidentally, the church's old piano was given to Glade Spring's senior citizens' center.)

An Organ Comes to Ebenezer

As mentioned earlier, my piano playing began in the 1950s. Over the years, I became more and more comfortable performing; however, my experience with organs was limited. No black churches in Glade Spring had an organ. The only black churches in Washington County with an organ *then* were Valley Street Baptist and Charles Wesley Methodist in Abingdon. Back in the 1960s or 1970s, Mrs. S. L. Hall, musician at Valley Street Baptist Church, gave me a few minutes of organ instruction. After this introduction, my next encounter with the organ came in the 1980s when I was asked to play for a funeral in Chilhowie. The Williams Funeral Home only had an organ. Because Mom had at one time worked for the Williams family, she asked one of the owners if it would be OK for me to practice a few minutes the day before the service. I managed to play very well the next day. Over the next decade, I was asked to play for a few more funerals—both in Abingdon and Chilhowie. During this period of time, these funeral homes only had organs.

The thought of having an organ at Ebenezer United Methodist Church had never really occurred to me. After all, my knowledge of this complicated instrument was limited, and I was not a trained musician. During my Christmas break in December of 2003, I considered buying a small organ for my home (I moved back to Glade Spring in 2001 to take care of Mom). I felt that if I had an organ at home and could practice occasionally, then my playing at those funeral homes would be less stressful. Oddly enough, I could not find any local outlets that sold organs of any size!

A few days later, I just happened to notice in *The Call* (a local Methodist church publication) that an area church had an old organ to sell for about $100; I also noticed that Emory & Henry College had an organ it wanted to give away! I was so surprised! Could this be something that I should pursue? I decided to call Anita Coulthard, the college's organist, to get more details. She indicated that a 1960-era organ had been locked up in an upstairs room in Byars Hall for a number of years and that the music faculty had decided to give it away. I decided to see this vintage musical instrument. My first impression was that the organ did not look very good. The wood finish was weather worn, one of the notes was broken, it did *not* play, and it had vacuum tubes inside. Moreover, getting this large musical machine out of its present location might be difficult.

Anita suggested that I get a keyboard specialist from Bristol to come to the college and determine if he could get the instrument to play again. Mr. Hobbs, the specialist, determined that he could make the organ work for about $250. I immediately decided that I would pay to have this organ moved to Ebenezer Church to be "brought back to life."

By the time Emory & Henry reconvened in January of 2004, I did not have a clue how I was going to get this big organ out of the Byars Hall room, which was on the top floor. There were no elevators in the building then! Someone suggested contacting a moving company in Kingsport—a company that had previously done some work in Byars Hall. Therefore, by early February, the organ was moved to Ebenezer, and Mr. Hobbs performed his electronic magic a few weeks later. My friend Clyde Tolliver came to the church to sand, stain, and varnish the wood. I used gorilla glue to repair the broken note. By the spring break in March 2004, Ebenezer United Methodist had its first organ. It looked good! It sounded good! Amen! Amen!

Even though I had spent about $1000 to get the organ in place, working, and looking like new, I was still somewhat apprehensive. Could I learn to play this instrument? Anita Coulthard gave me words of encouragement. "Just keep at it." I paid caregivers to stay with Mom so that I could go to the church to practice, practice, practice!

By April of 2004, I made plans to have a musical program to celebrate the giving of the organ to Ebenezer Church. Dirk Moore, the director of public relations at Emory & Henry College, visited me at the church and took pictures. He wrote an article about the church and its history, the giving of the organ by the college, and the upcoming dedicatory service. This article was posted to the school's website and appeared in an alumni magazine.

Dirk also contacted the *Bristol Herald Courier*. When a newspaper reporter called me, he indicated that his plan was to run a feature article in the religion section of a Saturday edition. However, on a Monday afternoon, April 12, at about 2:30 p.m., this reporter (Chris Dumond) called and informed me that a Tuesday morning story had fallen through. He wanted to come to Glade Spring within an hour and interview me—the church article to run the next day! I thought that it would be impossible to get a story together that quickly. But to my amazement, the interview and pictures were finished before 4:30 p.m. To my greater amazement, our story (including color pictures of me at the organ) appeared on the front page of the paper the next day! The story was picked up by wire services and appeared in a number of newspapers—*Roanoke Times*, *Richmond Times Dispatch*, and others.

While making last-minute preparations for the special dedicatory service scheduled for Sunday, April 18, I received a phone call. Our pastor, Emory & Henry student Josh Kilbourne, indicated that a WCYB television news crew was on its way to the church to profile the service! This profile appeared on the Sunday evening newscast. All of this publicity was unbelievable.

The Emory & Henry Connection

Over the years, a number of preachers at Ebenezer Church studied at Emory & Henry College—usually part time. In the 1960s, EHC student Harvey Johnson preached at our church and at Mt. Pleasant, an all-black church in Marion, Virginia. In the 1970s, William Weldon was studying at Emory & Henry while serving as pastor at Ebenezer and Charles Wesley churches. As mentioned earlier, Ebenezer's first white preacher was Emory senior Laura Blair from Abingdon, Virginia. There was an established bond between the overwhelmingly white Methodist college (Emory & Henry) and Glade Spring's overwhelmingly black Methodist church (Ebenezer).

At the 2001 Annual Conference for the Holston United Methodist Church, Ebenezer's pastor, John Roe, was reassigned. During that summer, Ebenezer did not have a pastor. A number of preachers served on a temporary basis. The UMC Abingdon district superintendent informed me in August that an Emory & Henry student was interested in serving at Ebenezer. The irony of this situation was that I was beginning my first year of teaching at the college. Sophomore Josh Kilbourne and I met one day in my computer classroom and made arrangements to meet at a Glade Spring fast-food establishment—then to travel to the "little church across the tracks."

Although Josh was very young at the time, I got the feeling that there was something special in his personality—a maturity beyond his years and a calling for the ministry. This was just what Ebenezer needed. In our one-on-one discussions, I discovered that Josh was from a family of Methodist ministers—his father having graduated from Emory and having become a preacher in several Holston Conference churches. Additionally, there were other family members who were (or had been) preachers. At the same time, Josh's uncle was a member of the business faculty at Emory; his office was down the hall from mine. Frequently, Ebenezer was visited by Kilbourne family members. We got to know his mother, father, brothers, grandparents, and others. Emory & Henry students also attended. The relationship between the historic college and the historic church had never been stronger. Moreover, the racial diversity of our church—the church that had started more than one hundred years earlier as an all-black place of worship—had become one of the most racially integrated churches in Washington County.

Because the membership of Ebenezer continued to be small, Josh made a point of visiting the various family homes. At this point in time, my mother's health was not very good. There were emergency room visits, and there were extended hospital stays. Both Josh and his grandmother visited Mom in the hospital. Knowing that I was having a hard time coping with my many personal and professional responsibilities, it was not uncommon for him to pray for me and to offer words of reassurance—both publicly and privately. When Josh graduated from Emory & Henry in 2004, his younger brother Nathan became Ebenezer's pastor from 2004 to 2006. Kilbourne family members and EHC students continued to visit our church—both for morning services and for special afternoon musical celebrations.

At about the same time that Nathan started his pastorate, David Montgomery, a local African-American soloist, started attending Ebenezer. He had grown up in Glade Spring's Plum Creek area, had been a frequent visitor at our church, and was upset when his own church—Plum Creek Baptist—suddenly closed. He had occasionally helped me with my mother's care. It was at this point in time that I decided to create a singing group for Ebenezer, a group consisting of David, Virginia Lockhart, and myself. Over a period of two years, we had many singing engagements throughout the region. At one point, we traveled to Wythe County to sing in the church were Laura Blair Wyke was then pastor. We tried several of the new gospel songs—"Total Praise," "I Can't Hold Back," "It's Good to Know Jesus," "Jesus, the Sweetest Name I Know," and "What a Marvelous Thing." I used a keyboard and electronic technology to augment my piano playing, and David and Virginia both brought to the forefront their many years of church music singing experiences. Virginia, originally from North Carolina and the daughter of a minister, came from a family with a rich background in African-American church music. Additionally, there were times when Nathan and several of his Emory & Henry friends joined our small singing group. We were even asked to perform at Emory & Henry events.

In January of 2006, Interim President Douglass Covington became the first African-American leader of Emory & Henry College. Early in his brief tenure at the college, Dr. Covington expressed his desire to visit our historic little church—a church that had been built by former slaves. This historic presidential event occurred in the spring of 2006. Dr. Covington and his entourage, along with students, community leaders, and friends, visited our morning services. Nathan Kilbourne preached, and our singing group presented special music. This was such an emotional experience for me. I was so proud of Ebenezer!

The Emory & Henry connection continues primarily because of the support of organist Anita Coulthard, religion professors, and others. Whenever we have one of our special afternoon singing events, she brings a group of singers to participate—singers often representing Emory and Meadowview United Methodist churches.

The author at his first piano, 1957.

Ebenezer United Methodist Church, Glade Spring, 2004.

The author playing the organ, Ebenezer United Methodist Church, Glade Spring, 2004.
Photo courtesy: Earl Neikirk, Bristol Herald Courier.

CHAPTER 7:
Work Experiences

Baltimore: First Teaching Job

WHEN I GRADUATED from Virginia State College in June of 1969, I had no idea how difficult it would be to find a job. One component of my financial package was the Virginia teachers loan—a financial aid plan that I'd had for all four years of study. The requirement of the loan was that it would be cancelled if the recipient taught in a public school in the state.

Over the course of the summer, I typed scores of letters—seeking applications for a teaching job in the Old Dominion. There were some school districts that did not respond to my query. One such district was my home county of Washington! There were a few districts that contacted me for interviews—Richmond, Roanoke, and Alexandria. When I got to the interviews, I was informed that there were no vacancies and that being interviewed was a routine part of the application process. With the summer rapidly coming to an end, I still could not find any high school teaching positions anywhere in the entire state of Virginia. Desperation was fast descending upon me. Was this a situation of there not being any openings for business teachers anywhere in the state? Or was this a situation of certain school districts not wanting to consider a recent honor graduate of the predominantly black Virginia State College?

Gradually, I started sending letters outside of Virginia—West Virginia and Maryland. Of course, if I got a job in one of these states, I would be required to repay the Virginia teachers loan. Although I was only twenty-one years old at the time, my maturity level was such that I felt like these circumstances were unfair!

By mid-August, I received a call from the Baltimore City Public School System. The caller requested that I come for an interview. Fearing that I was not experienced enough to drive my little car on the streets of this large city, I decided to drive to the Richmond-Petersburg area and take a Greyhound bus to Maryland.

The interview went well. The interviewer seemed to be impressed with my title ("Mr. Future Business Teacher"—Virginia, 1968) and with the fact that I had already earned several graduate credits during the just-ended summer (credits earned from East Tennessee State University—not far from my Glade Spring home). I was offered a job to teach at Dunbar High in Baltimore's inner city.

My brother, Bobby, who had some knowledge of Baltimore, felt that this school would be too tough for me. But I needed a job—any job! However, just days before I was scheduled to leave for Baltimore, I received a call from the school board headquarters. The caller indicated that my school assignment had been changed—from Dunbar to Eastern, an all-female school. (Historically, Eastern was one of the oldest public, all-female high schools in the entire country.) The reason for the school assignment change was the fact that Eastern was going to start a data processing curriculum. Even though I had only one computer class from my Virginia State College studies, this one course was enough for the Baltimore school administrators to believe that I should be a part of this innovative curriculum project! In retrospect, I am convinced that this school change was another case of divine intervention—the start of a teaching career in the area of computer literacy and programming.

My knowledge of Baltimore was limited. For example, I did not know that prior to integration, there were only two high schools for black students in the entire city—Douglass for the western district and Dunbar for the eastern district. However, this northern city technically ended segregation shortly after the 1954 Supreme Court *Brown v. Board of Education* ruling. The racial makeup of Baltimore public schools in 1969, however, would be something that I would soon discover firsthand.

Shortly before leaving Glade Spring, I traded my 1960 Ford for a 1967 Chevrolet. On my initial trip to Baltimore, I discovered that this car was mechanically defective. It was losing oil so badly that on my first fuel stop, the gas station attendant discovered that the engine oil chamber was almost empty! After oil and gas refills, I pressed onward to Baltimore.

My salary for 1969-1970 in Baltimore was $7000, and the school year was for ten months. I made arrangements to stay at the YMCA, which was located on Druid Hill Avenue in the heart of the city. The neighborhoods were very segregated—rows and rows of attached houses, apartment buildings, and projects—all inhabited primarily by black people. Several attempts to find an apartment near the school proved unsuccessful. Whenever I talked with prospective landlords on the phone, things seemed to go smoothly. But when I met with them, suddenly I got the cold shoulder treatment and a declaration that actually there were no vacancies!

Shortly after my arrival in Baltimore, two things occurred that related to my selective service status—I completed a physical, and the school superintendent wrote a letter to the draft board describing the difficulty in getting college graduates willing to teach in inner-city schools.

When I got to Eastern High, located on Thirty-Third Street across from Memorial Stadium, I found this very large school to be in a state of transition. Most of the faculty members and staff were white, and most of the students were black. Because the students were all female, most of the faculty and staff were also female. As a new employee, I ended up being in a minority status on several obvious levels—male, young, and black! There was an element of uneasiness that I sensed in this school—an uneasiness that was difficult for me to understand. After all, Baltimore's public school segregation had officially ended in the 1950s. Naively, I thought that by 1969, racial harmony should be commonplace!

As a probationary teacher at Eastern High School, my teaching load was very heavy—data processing, office machines, typewriting, and bookkeeping. The enrollment in one of the bookkeeping classes was about thirty-eight. The data processing class, a new offering, involved instruction using some old unit-record (punch card) machines that had been donated to the school system by area businesses.

- Accounting machine, collator, and interpreter were programmed by wiring panel boards.
- There were the requisite card-punching machines and a card sorter.
- The IBM reference manuals were overly technical.
- There were some easy-to-follow reference manuals written by a California-based author named Thomas Cashman.

The Eastern High School data processing curriculum was scheduled to be expanded—programming was soon to be taught on the IBM Model 1130. Accordingly, there were after-school in-service training sessions scheduled for several of us business teachers. The sessions were on RPG programming and were taught by a programmer/analyst from IBM. This was my first experience with computer programming centering on the use of the punch-card system.

The transition to city living was a challenge for me. I was not used to living in an all-black neighborhood. I also did not like staying at the YMCA and having to travel great distances just to find something to eat. There were no food service facilities at this branch of the Y, and I often ate dinner at the Greyhound bus station cafeteria and lunch in the high school cafeteria. Breakfast consisted of instant orange juice and cold cereal with powdered milk. I drove to an integrated suburb on weekends just to shop, to visit a laundry, and to reminisce about life back in Glade Spring!

Built in 1936, Eastern High School was one of the largest schools I had ever seen. As mentioned earlier, this school was located directly across the street from Baltimore's Memorial Stadium, and for each of the three years of my teaching at this school, World Series baseball games were played there—Orioles vs. New York Mets in 1969, Orioles vs. Cincinnati Reds in 1970, and Orioles vs. Pittsburgh Pirates in 1971. Of course, Eastern was in session during the home games.

For me, the defining incident at Eastern High School occurred in February of 1970. The incident began with verbal attacks between a white teacher and a black student. As the incident spread and violence presumably occurred, we teachers were instructed via intercom to keep our students in their current classrooms and to lock the door! The police were called, and eventually everyone was sent home. I never did get all of the details about what happened. But even though this incident took place more than forty years ago, it is something that I will never forget. Nothing in my young life—no college courses and no life experiences—had prepared me for this.

This incident (or riot) was covered on all Maryland radio and television stations and was printed in state newspapers. A wire service picked up the story and broadcast details to a few stations outside of Maryland. One radio station that carried this story was WBBI-AM in Abingdon, Virginia, and my mother happened to be listening to this station while at work in the Glade Spring home of Robert Porterfield. I was so shocked when she called me at the YMCA shortly after I got home following the abbreviated school day. Although she sometimes called me there, I was certain that she was calling about something else and knew nothing about the incident. I soon learned otherwise! She said that she had heard about the riot at Eastern High School and wanted to know if I was OK! It was at this point in time that I was unsure if I had made the right choice in coming to Baltimore to teach.

In the aftermath of the student unrest at Eastern High School, a number of changes occurred. Some teachers were reassigned, and sensitivity training was mandated for faculty, staff, and students. A few teachers even quit. By the start of the next school year, the white principal had been permanently replaced by a black principal.

Aside from the fact that work was proving to be stressful, my living arrangement in the YMCA was also problematic. My car, a 1970 model that had replaced the mechanically defective 1967 model, was broken into on more than one occasion. Many personal items were stolen.

In the summer of 1970, I was unsure if I would return to Baltimore. But because there were still no Virginia teaching jobs to be found, I made the decision to return to Eastern High School. At least the data processing training was proving to be very interesting. During the academic year of 1970-1971, I made preliminary plans to return to Virginia State College for graduate study. One of my Baltimore supervisors interjected that I should study in Maryland, but I had no desire to do so. Professor Mundon at VSC was very receptive to my inquiry about returning to study in Petersburg.

With the help of Uncle Arthur, I managed to find a new place to live—a place much closer to Eastern High School. The home was that of an elderly lady by the name of Helen Roberts. Her residence, near Morgan State College, was a place where Uncle Bascom had stayed while attending this college several decades earlier.

The second and third years at Eastern High School were better. Student unrest was nonexistent. The workload, however, did not decrease. I was asked to be school treasurer, as well as co-advisor to the class of 1972. I existed on no more than four or five hours of sleep each night. By the end of the 1971-1972 school year, all details for my graduate study at Virginia State College had been completed; I would study there full time for the 1972-1973 academic year.

With my master's degree completed, I returned to Baltimore for the 1973-1974 academic year. Instead of returning to Eastern High School, I was reassigned to Walbrook Senior High. Walbrook was then a new school, having been completed in 1971. It was located in the western part of Baltimore. Therefore, I called again on Uncle Arthur to help me find a place to live near the school. I rented a room from another elderly lady.

At Walbrook High, I continued to teach data processing and other business courses. The most noteworthy event to occur during my tenure at Walbrook was a citywide teachers' strike. For the second time in my young teaching career, I was confronted with a situation for which I was unprepared. As a probationary teacher living in a city where I had no relatives, I could not join in the strike; I had no financial resources to do so. The strike went on for weeks, and there were reported incidences of violence and property damage—strikers against non-strikers. Because my car still had Virginia tags, many picketing teachers perhaps assumed that I commuted from Virginia daily. For this reason, I believe no one bothered to pursue my place of residence. Although there were several angry looks, I escaped violence and vandalism. It was at this point in time that I was determined to get out of Baltimore. Perhaps in 1974 there would be a job for me somewhere in my home state.

While studying at Virginia State College in Petersburg during the 1972-1973 academic year, many of us in the graduate programs heard much about the Virginia Community College System. A major headline was that a new community college in the Richmond area was in its infant stages and that rapid expansion was forthcoming. In the winter of 1974, I made two trips to Richmond for job interviews—at Virginia Union University and at J. Sargeant Reynolds Community College. Both interviews were scheduled on holidays when the Baltimore schools were closed. I had no plans to broadcast my plans of leaving Maryland. The community college salary offer was higher. I accepted.

The Baltimore teachers' strike had a major impact on the remaining school year. Usually the summer vacation began in early June. However, in the spring of 1974, we were informed that the academic year would be extended close to July—making up the lost time. I was very upset with this scheduling. I was scheduled to participate in the commencement exercises at VSC, receiving my master's degree. I decided that I would not go because of the pressures of the Baltimore teaching job and the longevity of the school year. Secretly, I knew that I would not be returning to this city in the fall and that my teaching career would be significantly different. The role of college professor would be a new challenge.

Richmond: Second Teaching Job

When I went to Richmond to be interviewed for a job at J. Sargeant Reynolds, the college was temporarily operating in a converted furniture store building in the heart of the city. The first permanent structure was under construction. This new building was located in suburban Henrico county. My interviewer, Dr. Robert Bowers, indicated that I would be teaching at this location.

The start of the school year (1974-1975) at JSRCC had to be delayed by one week, because the new building in Henrico County was not finished. This building, located on Parham Road, was in the final stages of completion—so we were told. When we got to this building, there were classrooms with no doors or ceilings and laboratory rooms that were not yet furnished. As faculty, we were called on to join in and help with a variety of custodial duties.

When I think back to my first quarter of college teaching, the first thing that comes to mind was how much I felt at ease. By contrast, my days as a high school teacher required me to assume the role of ultimate disciplinarian—a role with which I was not very comfortable. At J. Sargeant Reynolds, I felt very relaxed in the classroom. My sense of humor started to surface. This humor was readily accepted by many students who had the preconceived notion that computer classes would be very dry and very boring. As a result of my classroom demeanor, I started to get high student evaluations. It was at this point in time I realized that the hardships I had endured in Baltimore had prepared me for the enjoyment that I was currently experiencing. What a great life lesson!

In the first year at J. Sargeant Reynolds Community College, I was the only full-time computer teacher on our campus. Another computer teacher, Linda Scott Whippo, had been hired earlier but was involved in teaching other business-related courses. The plan was for her to move to the computer area in the 1975-1976 school year, as the enrollment at the new Parham Road campus was expected to increase significantly. For a few years, the two of us (augmented by some part-time instructors) ran the campus data processing program.

In addition to Linda Whippo, there were many faculty and staff members in the business division that became instant friends in those early years. Familiar names included Keith Wells, Doris Patterson Bland, Doug Cobbs, JoAnn Sherron, Deborah Gray Canada, Barbara Comfort, Charles Reynolds, Jane Williams, Lea Emory, Gary Denby, Willnette Foley, Bob Yancey, Catherine Small, and several others. Because he had a close friend who lived in Abingdon, Keith Wells, an accounting instructor in the mid-1970s, actually visited my Glade Spring home one summer—the only JSRCC faculty person to do so. Ethnically speaking, the number of black faculty on the Parham Road campus was minimal during those early years. In the business division, for example, there were only three of us who served for several years—Doris Patterson Bland, Doug Cobbs, and myself.

For several years at J. Sargeant Reynolds Community College, my primary teaching responsibility was teaching introductory computer classes, programming logic, and COBOL programming. All of these courses were very exciting even though the area of data processing (later named information systems) was not as widespread as today. For example, in the early days, there were no microcomputers—only the mainframe and the related card-punching equipment. At one point, I taught an accounting course.

The student body at the Parham Road campus of JSRCC was diverse. Not only were there many African-American and white students, there were often many students who had come to America from a number of foreign countries. Many times, I jokingly referred to some of my classes as "United Nations" classes. Moreover, a number of JSRCC students had physical challenges—visual, hearing, mobility, and so forth. The college, in my opinion, did an excellent job in accommodating the various needs of these students.

The downtown campus (where I never taught) had a higher percentage of black students than the Parham road campus. Over the years, I came to realize the closeness that often existed between faculty and students, especially the adult students. They visited our offices often. Not only did they discuss their coursework, but they often talked about their personal lives—their families, their work, their problems, and other life experiences. I found this to be very engaging.

Unlike my experiences in Baltimore, I did not have a problem finding a place to live in Richmond. The apartment building in which I lived was in a racially diverse midtown neighborhood and was near an interstate highway. Although it was not a luxurious building, it suited my needs very well. I lived in the same building (three different apartments) for each of my Richmond years. I spent the summer months primarily in Glade Spring.

In the early years of my teaching at the Richmond-based community college, there were many opportunities for additional study and workshops. The computer curriculum was always changing—usually very fast. For some reason, however, I felt that I wanted to get another college degree. Even though a master's degree was sufficient for teaching at the community-college level, there were a number of us at JSRCC who began to talk about earning a doctoral degree. At first, I discounted this notion, because I felt that my background was such that this would be difficult. Interestingly, in the early 1970s, Virginia Tech in Blacksburg had started educational doctoral programs—programs that could be completed with a minimum amount of time at the home campus. The idea that I could actually study at Virginia Tech—another historically white school founded back in the post-Civil-War era—was certainly something that was intriguing to me. In 1975, I decided to pursue my EdD degree at Virginia Tech in the area of vocational-technical education. Because I had already completed a number of graduate courses at East Tennessee State, Morgan State, and Virginia State, my coursework total was sufficiently high. Many of my colleagues at JSRCC enrolled in many of the Virginia Tech graduate courses—courses that were offered at off-campus sites, such as Virginia Beach, Northern Virginia, and Richmond.

In the summer of 1976, I stayed at the Virginia Tech campus in Blacksburg and completed three courses. By 1977-1978, I was ready to study full time at the Blacksburg campus in order to satisfy the residency requirement. JSRCC awarded me an educational leave of absence for this purpose. The degree was completed in 1979.

In the early 1980s, another life-changing event occurred while teaching at JSRCC. One of my courses was called Flowcharting and Computer Programming Logic. Our school had written the course description, and it was used statewide. Because of a shift in the emphasis of this course, we found it necessary to change the textbook that had been used for several years; structured programming logic was the new emphasis. The textbook selected, although covering this new topic, was poorly written. Book representatives visited faculty often, and when one of these representatives came to my office, she asked me to describe the textbook currently used that I disliked the most! I proceeded to berate this programming logic book, but I did not realize that this book was published by her company. As we continued with our conversation, she made the suggestion that I write my own book on this topic. Therefore, in 1986, my textbook (*Structured Programming Logic: A Flowcharting Approach*) was published by Prentice Hall, Incorporated. This book was used by a number of colleges, including JSRCC, for a few years.

Over my several years at JSRCC, I was regularly promoted—starting as assistant professor and then on to associate and full professor. In the early 1980s, I tried a few times to teach short-term classes during the summer sessions. My personal preference, however, was to spend downtime in Glade Spring. Often I was asked to teach several classes off campus—local middle schools, high schools, and businesses. On one occasion, I traveled several miles to a rural Virginia county—Fluvanna. There I taught a programming logic course at Fork Union Military Academy. The enrollees were faculty and staff at the school. For a period of time in the late 1980s, I taught computer courses on a part-time basis at Richmond's Marymount High School.

As the enrollments increased in the area of information systems, JSRCC instituted a policy known as "cross-training." Several faculty members who were teaching in a variety of low-enrollment disciplines were enrolled in computer classes. This occurred for several years, especially at the Parham Road campus. As a result, many of the long-serving members of the information-system area had originally taught other courses at the school. After a while, I got used to having faculty members taking my courses!

One situation at our community college—a situation that more than likely occurred at other schools at the time—was the faculty evaluation process, a process that I felt did not take into account the volatile nature of the information-systems curriculum area. Our subject matter was constantly changing—often at lightning speed. However, we were held to the same evaluative standards as faculty members who taught in disciplines that changed more slowly. We were always expected to be innovative in our teaching methodology even though our content mastery was ongoing.

By the late 1990s, my travel between Richmond and Glade Spring increased, primarily because of my mother's declining health. By 1998, I was determined to retire from the Virginia Community College System and move back home. I spent the 1998-1999 sabbatical year in Glade and returned to Richmond on a regular basis.

Many people in Glade Spring, especially the black community, knew of my mother's declining health, and they also knew that I was planning to return home as soon as possible to take care of her. However, the earliest that I could leave Richmond was 2001. The stipulation of my sabbatical award was that I must complete two additional years at J. Sargeant Reynolds.

Some of the questions in my mind had to do with finances. How would I take care of Mom and live on my Virginia retirement salary? Would I be able to find a part-time job? If so, what and where would this part-time job be? Should I end my teaching career? Would I be able to find paid help to assist in Mom's care? For many reasons, I was not comfortable with the idea of putting her in a nursing home! I had an established relationship between Virginia Highlands Community College (Abingdon); I had done my doctoral internship there in 1977 and had also done some volunteer work there as a part of my sabbatical year. Perhaps I could teach there. Would this even be the right thing to do? After so many years of living in Richmond, would I feel culturally lost in Southwest Virginia—no black radio stations, no black news anchors or reporters on local television, and greater emphasis by local media on Tennessee news than Virginia news? Would I make new friends? Could I reconnect with old friends? There were so many questions, and I had few answers.

During the summer of 2000, I received a call that—in retrospect—was another life-changing event. The call was from Ann Hill, an African-American Glade Spring native and the daughter of Robert and Elizabeth Hill. Ann, an attorney and graduate of Emory & Henry College, was then a member of the college's board of trustees. In her phone call, she mentioned that she had heard that I planned to retire from my Richmond job in 2001. She asked if I had ever considered teaching at Emory! I was in a mild state of shock—not because I did not think that Emory was a great school, but because I could not imagine that my vocational-technical education background was something that had a place at this liberal arts college. Nevertheless, she suggested that I send her a copy of my resume, which she planned to forward to President Tom Morris.

When I met with President Morris a few months later, I was even more astonished to learn that the college was planning to start a three-credit computer literacy course in the fall of 2001—a course that was similar to one I had been teaching at JSRCC for years! After our meeting and a subsequent meeting with the dean of faculty, Paul Blaney, plans were initiated for me to become an adjunct professor at Emory & Henry beginning in the fall of 2001!

With one more year remaining at JSRCC, I made plans to get the retirement paperwork set in motion. Fortunately, I was able to buy my Maryland retirement service and to add on to the Virginia service. With a year of unused sick leave, I would be able to leave the Virginia Community College System with the *equivalent* of thirty-two years of service.

At the risk of sounding overly philosophical, I felt that all of these developments were somehow meant to be—that my years of living, working, and studying in other regions had prepared me for this time in my life—a time *still* filled with personal challenges and struggles, but also filled with rewards, growth, and a sense of making a difference.

The author teaching at Eastern High School, Baltimore, 1969.

The author teaching at J. Sargeant Reynolds Community College, Richmond, 1980s.

CHAPTER 8:
Graduate and Continuing Education

TO GAIN AN extra edge in getting my first high school teaching job, I enrolled in my first graduate courses during the summer following my graduation from Virginia State College. These courses were at East Tennessee State University in Johnson City—roughly forty miles from Glade Spring. For ten weeks in the summer of 1969, I traveled daily to this university and took courses in business administration and education. I also attended ETSU briefly in the summer of 1970 and again during the summer of 1971. Instead of traveling daily from Glade Spring to Johnson City that last summer, I stayed in Bristol during the week and only went home on the weekends—staying at a motel that was located across the street from Bristol's former Douglass High School. During my second year in Baltimore (1970-1971), I enrolled in Morgan State College (now Morgan State University) and completed two semesters of cost accounting.

At East Tennessee State, I was one of only two or three black students in my classes, and at Morgan State, then a predominately black school, my graduate cost accounting class consisted of only five students. Two of us were black, as was the adjunct professor. The other students were natives of other countries.

All of this coursework was beneficial; however, there was a need for computer classes beyond the in-service training received from the Baltimore City School System. It was at this point in time that I decided to return to Virginia State College to reside full time and to get a master's degree in business education. In the early 1970s, however, there were computer courses but not a degree in programming or information systems.

After completing three years of teaching in Baltimore, I applied for and was granted an educational leave of absence to return to Petersburg in 1972. I also applied for and received a graduate assistantship from Virginia State, funding that helped me pay for my studies. Professor Ella Mundon was instrumental in helping me to get this assistantship.

Because of her assistance, I was also able to get a room on campus—staying in one of the men's dormitories.

Virginia State College had changed significantly in the three years since I received my bachelor's degree. Enrollment had grown, and the faculty and student body were more racially diverse. The business education department was still chaired by Professor Mundon, and the business education graduate program was run by Professor Marlene Simpson. My fellowship duties involved my working for both of these professors. I also did some work for Professor Ruby Hayes, a member of the accounting faculty.

As a part of my assistantship duties, I occasionally served as a substitute teacher in a teaching methodology class and a business English class. I regularly assisted Professor Simpson with her office procedures class.

When Professor Simpson went back to Columbia University in the spring semester to finish her doctoral degree, my graduate advisor became Dr. Don Campbell, assisted by newly hired Dr. Patricia Wells—white professors who were adding to Virginia State's new diverse faculty profile.

Many of the enrollees in Virginia State College's graduate division in 1972 were off-campus students—teachers in the surrounding counties who were seeking employment upgrades. Their racial profiles and teaching backgrounds were varied.

Two pivotal courses in my VSC graduate program involved computers—computer concepts and programming. Additionally, my master's project was an extension of this technology-specific coursework. All of this preparation was designed to be used in my high school teaching when I returned to Baltimore for the next school year. However, the degree emphasis on postsecondary teaching (i.e., community college teaching) was—in my opinion—an appropriate VSC focus. I never accepted the notion that teaching methodology was something that was inherently picked up. On the contrary, it is a skill that should be researched, studied, refined, and debated. In summary, my VSC graduate study involved the following courses:

    Public School Law

    Administration and Supervision in Business Education

    Foundations of Education

    Statistical Procedures

    Curriculum Development in Business Education

> Business Education in Postsecondary Schools
>
> COBOL Programming
>
> Computer Concepts
>
> A master's degree project

Even though I chose the master's project option instead of the thesis option, I was still required to present an oral defense. This defense was completed in the summer of 1973 (I made a round trip from Glade Spring to Petersburg all in one day—a total of nearly six hundred miles!)

When I moved to Richmond in 1974, I enrolled in a computer programming course at Virginia Commonwealth University. There were many workshops provided for business faculty to keep up with the ever-changing area of computer education. But, as mentioned in chapter 7 of this book, my decision in the mid-1970s to seek a doctoral degree at Virginia Tech was not specifically directed toward my immediate career objectives at the community college level. It was my personal belief that an advanced degree could only help my long-range objectives. Additionally, there was the ever-present knowledge of my background—the financial struggles of my early childhood, as well as the circumstances of my segregation-era public school education—that made me want to prove to myself that I could achieve this personal goal.

Graduate coursework at Virginia Tech was innovatively delivered. There were times when the university flew a professor to Richmond to teach a class on Friday afternoons and Saturday mornings. Some of us at JSRCC even traveled to Virginia Beach (about one and a half hours from Richmond) to take courses. However, the most extensive off-campus coursework was offered at a Northern Virginia site near Dulles International Airport. Many of us would drive to the site (about one and a half hours away) and take courses. The courses started at either 4:00 p.m. or 7:00 p.m. In the winter of 1977, I took Behavioral Science Methodology, and in the spring of 1977, I took Intermediate Statistics for Education—this class started at 7:00 p.m. I would get back to Richmond around midnight, teaching an 8:00 a.m. class at JSRCC the next morning. My early days of traveling to and from Douglass High School in Bristol had prepared me well for this type of scheduling!

The summer of 1976 was spent at the Blacksburg campus taking three courses. In summary, Virginia Tech coursework included some of the following titles:

Administration and Supervision in Vocational-Technical Education

History and Philosophy of Vocational-Technical Education

Community College Curriculum

Advanced Educational Psychology

College Teaching

Vocational-Technical Education for the Disadvantaged

Post-Secondary Vocational-Technical Education

Behavioral Science Methodology

Intermediate Statistics for Education

Business and Society

Concepts, Principles, and Practices of Career Education

By the fall of 1977, I was ready to study at the home campus of Virginia Tech in Blacksburg. I received an educational leave of absence from JSRCC to do so. This academic year consisted of coursework as well as the beginning phases of my dissertation. Virginia Tech classes, both off campus and on campus—were very racially diverse. Many African-American graduate students came from the Northern Virginia and Washington areas. As mentioned earlier, the student profiles from my East Tennessee State days a few years earlier were not so diverse. During my time at Virginia Tech, I had at least two African-American professors—a rare occurrence in my graduate studies (except at Virginia State and Morgan State).

My dissertation topic was entitled "An Analysis of Selected Variables Relating to Levels of Academic Performance of First-Year Computer Programming Students in Virginia Community Colleges." This research project required me to travel to a number of Virginia community colleges—travel that occurred during the spring of 1978. Although I visited about eight schools in order to conduct my research, I did not find any African-American computer educators at these institutions.

There are those who refer to a doctoral degree as a "terminal" degree! As a computer educator, I knew that this certainly was *not* going to be the case for me. With my Virginia Tech degree completed in June 1979, only a few years went by before I was taking additional courses. As mentioned in chapter 7, my involvement in the teaching of computer classes began in 1969 at Baltimore's Eastern High School. One of the problems in teaching such courses—especially in the early years—was that there were few good textbooks and lab manuals to use. In my Eastern High School data processing classes, I was fortunate to have some good lab manuals written by a California-based author by the name of Thomas Cashman. I continued to see that name on textbooks while I was working at Richmond's J. Sargeant Reynolds Community College. Upon receiving an advertisement that Cashman and other computer textbook authors would be conducting summer institutes specifically designed for computer educators, I was intrigued. Some of the initial institutes were held in Oklahoma, and by the early 1980s, they were being held at Memphis State University (now the University of Memphis).

Since I always spent summers at Mom's house in Glade Spring, I felt like the bordering state of Tennessee was close to me. The distance from Bristol to Memphis, however, was close to five hundred miles. Nevertheless, in the summer of 1982, I attended my first such conference (then named the Cashman and Keys Summer Institute). I studied COBOL programming, as well as associated teaching methodologies. This experience, which lasted two weeks and which awarded graduate credit, was very exciting to me. I studied at similar Memphis State institutes during the summers of 1985 and 1986—a grand total of nine graduate credits. Aside from the course content and teaching methodologies, interactions with fellow attendees—attendees with a wide range of experiences and from geographically dispersed locations—were very informative. Participants, always racially diverse, came from all across the United States. Additionally, the instructors—career teachers and authors—were outstanding. These summer learning experiences were rewarding to me, both personally and professionally. I flew to Memphis in 1982 (only my second plane trip ever), but I drove in 1985 and 1986 (about a ten-hour drive). I was fascinated to hear Tom Cashman talk about his background in business education.

After my first Memphis State summer institute in 1982, JSRCC would not pay for my tuition—citing the belief that this training should be received in Richmond. I decided to personally pay for these institutes, because I felt that the benefits were immeasurable. In my mind, the comparison between a national conference and a local seminar was not a subject worthy of debate!

In the late 1980s and early 1990s, the graduate school at Virginia State University in Petersburg decided to offer some short-term classes specifically designed for teachers. Of special interest to me were courses offered by the business education department. These courses covered computer topics—spreadsheets, word processing, and database formation and maintenance. Therefore, for three summers (1989, 1991, and 1993), I left Glade Spring and returned to my Richmond apartment for one week. Driving to Petersburg daily (about a thirty-minute drive), I completed these computer-content teacher workshops—workshops that each awarded three graduate credits.

Attendees at the workshops came from all across Virginia, including my native southwestern area.

It was great to return to the school that had awarded me both my bachelor's degree and master's degree only a few years earlier. Furthermore, I was honored to have as my first professor Dr. Marlene Simpson, who had been my graduate professor. My second teacher was Professor Peggy Lee, who, during my undergraduate days, was an administrative assistant in the School of Commerce. My third professor was Dr. Claiborne Shelton, a VSC business education undergraduate during the time period in which I was similarly classified. These training experiences, which I personally financed, were all very beneficial!

By the 1990s, the Cashman and Keys Summer Institutes had become the Shelly Cashman Summer Institutes. Gary Shelly, a one-time student of Tom Cashman, had become a coauthor with the publishing firm with which these authors were then affiliated. Moreover, the institutes were then being offered at Purdue University in West Lafayette, Indiana. I knew that Indiana was quite some distance from Virginia, and I was somewhat apprehensive about driving there. But prior institute experiences indicated to me that attending one of these Indiana-based conferences might be something that I should do.

For the summer of 1995, I traveled by car from Glade Spring to Indiana's Purdue University. The trip took approximately ten hours. I had carefully studied my route and had typed large sheets indicating the pivotal route changes to be made. Traveling through rural areas of Southwest Virginia was exciting, and driving through the state of Kentucky was equally pleasurable.

My knowledge of Purdue was limited; however, I remembered the name of this university from the old television show *College Bowl*, hosted by Allen Ludden from 1959 to 1962. The campus was very impressive. As expected, the summer institute was also impressive. I returned to Purdue in 1996, 1997, 1999, and 2000, participating in the Shelly Cashman Summer Institutes. A variety of subjects were covered—Visual Basic, Microsoft Office, Windows, web design, and many other dynamic, computer-related topics. Institute enrollments were usually high—often hundreds of teachers from across the country. In the year of 2000, however, I felt that this would be the last such conference I would attend. I knew that my teaching career was most likely coming to an end. Moreover, even if I were to teach a part-time course load when I returned to my hometown, I could not walk away from my mother's care for a whole week! Even though my brother and his wife were living in Bristol at the time, Mother refused to stay with them. I had assumed the role of primary caregiver—even in the years before I officially left my teaching position in Richmond.

As detailed in chapter 9 of this book, I did not leave my hometown area at all 2001 to 2005; I was Mom's caregiver until her death in 2005.

At the suggestion of my Cincinnati cousin, Rose Swain, I made the decision to return to summer study—returning to Purdue University in July of 2005 for yet another Shelly Cashman Summer Institute. This time, my purpose for attending was twofold—getting reacquainted with the latest computer software topics and getting out of Glade Spring in an effort to move beyond my mother's passing. My cousin gave excellent advice. This particular year, the conference was not held on the main Purdue campus; the location was slightly north of the buildings where we usually lived and studied. On the way back from Purdue, I stopped by Cincinnati and visited Rose—one of the few people who helped to get me through the loss of both my brother in 2001 and my mother in 2005!

In 2006, the Shelly Cashman Summer Institute was moved to Indiana University in Bloomington. This location was much closer to Glade Spring. By this time, I had been teaching at Emory & Henry College for a number of years. With EHC's emphasis on teacher evaluation, even for those of us who were *not* tenure-track professors, I concluded that the IU conference could be helpful in keeping my evaluative profile at a comparatively high level. Accordingly, I have returned to IU for a number of years.

I had forgotten that Indiana University was the location of world-famous sex researcher Alfred Kinsey. The Kinsey Institute is still on this very large campus. During that first year, we were allowed to tour this institute. Although this information was more sociologically based than computer based, I found it to be very informative. A movie profiling this researcher's life was also presented.

The Shelly Cashman Summer Institutes are currently sponsored by Cengage publishers. This company is a leader in the area of computer textbooks. Additionally, they present a variety of conferences and seminars in addition to the IU summer events. I have attended March conferences in Nevada and Florida.

Whenever I go to a Shelly Cashman Summer Institute, I am looked upon as one of the veteran attendees—starting at Memphis State, moving to Purdue, and now attending at Indiana University. There are several other participants who have also been attending for many years. It is always good to see them at these enriching events.

At Emory & Henry College, I was recently asked to become involved in the teaching of the new core curriculum—courses central to the stated mission of this nationally recognized liberal arts college. Accordingly, beginning in the summer of 2008, my continuing education took another dramatic turn. In order to teach the newly defined Transitions I course, a remake of the old freshman orientation class, it was necessary for me to take a series of faculty workshops that were designed to prepare faculty for teaching specific proficiencies—proficiencies that are described by some authors as "soft skills." Listed below are some of these skills that, at Emory & Henry College, are paramount:

    critical thinking—problem solving and decision making

    ethical reasoning—guiding the thought process in a *principled* way

    information literacy—using the library effectively

    oral communication—small- and large-group presentations; teamwork

    quantitative literacy—reasoning with numbers and associated concepts

    written communication—electronic and nonelectronic documentation

There were also numerous workshops that were designed to help teachers become effective student advisors; I participated in them all. My education pursuits, diverse and long ranging, continue to be joyful.

The author's graduation, Virginia Tech, 1979.
(Left to right) Bobby Jones, Helen Jones, Omega Waugh, and Willie Cooper (cousin).

Indiana University, summer of 2010.

CHAPTER 9:

At Home Again

LUCILLE BALL, RONALD Reagan, Mahalia Jackson, and Mary Waugh Jones—these four people have *what* in common? They were all born in 1911—a *trivial* fact that was embedded in my mind for years. By the time I made plans to return to Glade Spring, only my mother and Reagan were still alive, and they both were suffering from Alzheimer's disease.

In the late 1990s, my mother's health declined noticeably. As mentioned in earlier chapters, I decided to take a one-year sabbatical from my teaching job at J. Sargeant Reynolds Community College in Richmond, Virginia, and spend the year with her in Glade Spring (1998-1999 school year). She was eighty-seven at the time, and even though my brother and his wife were living in Bristol, Mom was living alone in the same house where she was born. I felt that she needed me. Dementia is so unpredictable!

One special church event occurred while I was spending my sabbatical year in Glade Spring. Martha K. Bowers, Marie Brown, and other members of Fairview Baptist Church asked me to be the keynote speaker for their annual Black History celebration. I worked for weeks preparing my speech. Mom, Bobby, and Helen joined me for this event. Because I had spent so many years playing piano in this and other area churches, it was so unusual to assume this *new* role of speaker and to be introduced by longtime friend Robert Hill Jr. True to my style of delivery in the classroom, I managed to inject some humor into the message that I delivered on a Sunday evening in February of 1999. Even though Mom was sometimes confused with her dementia condition, I recall her saying to me how much she enjoyed the speech. After so many years of being a teacher, I suddenly realized that she had never seen me in a classroom or in the role of guest speaker! (The next time all of the Joneses attended this Black History event was 2001; my brother was then the guest speaker, one of his last public appearances!)   The year went by quickly. There were a number of doctor visits and hospital stays, and essentially I assumed the role of primary caregiver—a role for which I felt so unprepared. (While Mom was in the Marion hospital, I spent each night in her room!) But one does what one has to do. I desperately wanted to retire from my Richmond job and move back to Glade Spring and care for her. But according to my college's employment guidelines, I was required to complete two years in exchange for being granted the sabbatical.

When August of 1999 arrived, I had no choice but to return to Richmond, realizing that I would be coming home several weekends a month. By teaching a large block of classes on Tuesdays and Thursdays (finishing at 10:00 p.m.) at JSRCC, I would be able to have some flexibility with my Monday and Friday work schedule—going home early on Fridays and returning on Monday afternoons. This allowed me to buy groceries on Saturdays, play for church on Sunday mornings, take Mom to doctor appointments on Monday mornings, and leave money in the house for the caregivers. I was also able to call in prescription refills to a local pharmacy so that my brother could pick them up and take to Mom's house. Often I would vary my Richmond-Glade routes—leaving the interstate highways often to keep from getting bored.

By the year 2000, my brother and I were able to find a few caregivers who would spend several hours a day in the Glade Spring home. There were the frequent visits by Bobby and Helen, as well as the numerous phone calls per day from all of us. Unfortunately, some caregivers were not very dependable. One left town and never gave any notice that she was quitting. One day, she just didn't show up! Overall, Mom's care was hit or miss. She refused to spend much time at my brother's Bristol home. Fortunately, the school year went by rather fast; summer of the year 2000 allowed me to be back at home. My retirement plans were primarily completed, and the caregiver situation was far more stable.

As mentioned in chapter 7, with the arrival of summer in 2000, there was some focus to my future plans. In 2001, I would be teaching part time at Virginia Highlands Community College and Emory & Henry College. Both schools would have me as an adjunct professor in the area of information systems. With several caregivers on a rotating basis, I felt more confident that my last Richmond school year would be OK.

In the early months of 2001, it became obvious that my brother Bobby was not well. His wife, Helen, and his stepson, William, both indicated their concerns. At first, I discounted these concerns, largely because I could not imagine that my brother was not taking care of his health. He always seemed to be on top of everything—the ultimate planner and organizer. Unfortunately, I soon discovered that I was wrong; he had not seen a medical doctor in years! By the spring of 2001, his weight loss was apparent, and the diagnosis was uncertain.   My retirement from my teaching job in Richmond was fast approaching; a retirement luncheon was scheduled for Linda Whippo and me, both of us having completed nearly thirty years of service at JSRCC. The school year officially ended the week after Mother's Day. Bobby died May 16, one day short of his sixty-fifth birthday. This was the same day that I drove in from Richmond with the last of my belongings. In retrospect, I know why I have waited so long to begin this book chapter! I have dreaded going through this difficult time in my life again. I lost my sibling, and I had to also deal with the uncertainty of singularly making all of the decisions with respect to Mom's care. I really didn't have much time to reflect about my upcoming career changes, personal life changes, or anything beyond the immediate moments.

The actual return to Glade Spring living was not as bad as I had originally imagined. By spending so much time at home during summers and holidays, the adjustments were minimal. Additionally, because I had always taken care to keep the old house in a fairly good state of repair, at least I did not have to immediately contend with fixing things. For a house that was then more than 130 years old, it was in fairly decent shape. And even though Mom's health was unpredictable, there were a lot of good times. In my first two years back home, we ate out often, and we explored country roads almost every Sunday afternoon. As mentioned in other chapters, I refocused my leadership role at Ebenezer United Methodist Church. Mom and I also frequently visited other churches (e.g., Fairview Baptist and Plum Creek Baptist) when they scheduled special Sunday afternoon services.

People often recall the life circumstances surrounding certain memorable events in history. For example, in an earlier chapter, references were made to our Douglass High School activities on November 22, 1963, the day when President John Kennedy was assassinated. References were made in another chapter about my Virginia State College activities when Dr. Martin Luther King was assassinated in April 1968. A reference must now be made about the activities of September 11, 2001. This was my first semester of teaching at Virginia Highlands Community College and Emory & Henry College. During that first year, all of my classes were on Mondays, Wednesdays, and Fridays. I did *not* have any caregivers for my mother on Tuesdays and Thursdays. Therefore, for any errands I had to complete on those two days, it was necessary to take my mother with me. On this particular day in September of 2001, a Tuesday, I found it necessary to go to VHCC to make copies of a test to be given the next day. Mom was in a faculty office with me when news came about the terrorist activities. It had been ten years since my mother and I had been in the Pentagon, the occasion being my brother's retirement from government service. My mother's mental condition, however, prevented her from grasping the nature of the events of that horrific day.

One hometown adjustment had to do with scheduling—getting up every morning at 4:30 a.m. to prepare Mom's meals and medicines for the day. When caregivers arrived, I had everything ready, including Mom cleaned, dressed, hair appropriately combed, and ready to receive the breakfast I had prepared. Additionally, everything in the house, including the kitchen, was in order. Incidentally, the preparation of medicines and vitamins was uniquely challenging. Because Mom could not swallow pills, I had to crush them and then mix them with syrup and ice cream. If this mixture was placed in the freezer by 5:00 a.m., the consistency was just right when the caregiver arrived at 8:00 a.m.

I was able to find music that I liked—installing a satellite radio in my car, truck, and home; similarly, Mom's TV cable subscription was expanded to include premium channels like Showtime. There was a program on this channel to which I was addicted. I found that black gospel music had advanced significantly while I was busy traveling so often between Richmond and Glade Spring. Some of this music provided the uplift that was greatly needed as I went about my daily tasks of teaching college classes, caring for a parent, running a household, and running a church.

Aside from regular doctor visits, I made a point of taking Mom to a hairdresser in Bristol on a regular basis; I felt that it was important for her to look her best. I also bought her new clothes when I thought it was appropriate to do so. One of Mom's doctors was African-American—Dr. Renee Mason of Abingdon's Foot & Ankle Clinic. When she learned of my plans to write this book, Dr. Mason was so kind as to send me an e-mail detailing some of the problems she and her husband, Dr. Brian Mazzei, encountered when they moved to this area to practice medicine—a move which was in the post-segregation era of the 1990s. The stated notion by some area "establishment" medical providers was that blacks and whites of this area *always* got along. The belief of many (including myself) is that "getting along" is *more* than mere *tolerance*, staying in one's place, or accepting the status quo!

My most memorable experience with Dr. Mason was her comment about how well my mother was always dressed when I brought her in for office visits. I could not imagine that this was something that had been noticed. I felt so honored!

By far, my most uplifting Southwest Virginia "rebirth" resulted in my working as a teacher at Virginia Highlands Community College and Emory & Henry College. I had no idea that I would be so well received at these two schools. Because my previous work experiences had been with such large institutions, the smallness of VHCC and EHC was exactly what I needed at this point in my career. After one academic year (2001-2002), Emory & Henry wanted me on a more permanent basis; therefore, I ended my teaching at Virginia Highlands. By the start of the 2002-2002 academic year, my title at EHC became *Visiting* Professor in Computer Information Management—the only professor in that discipline area. I became the campus computer literacy person. Additionally, I was *then* the only African-American faculty member. After ten years, I am still "visiting" and am considered to be the longest-serving, highest-ranking African-American faculty member at the college.

By the 2003-2004 academic year, Mom's caregiver situation improved significantly. Dorothy Tolliver, a resident of Emory (near the college's campus), had a special ability when it came to my mother's care. In addition, her ability to stay for extended hours was unbelievable. I was able to have a greater presence on campus, attending late-afternoon faculty meetings regularly. I was also able to spend some time at Ebenezer Church, supervising the many physical improvements that I was funding (see chapter 6). I would drive to Kingsport, Tennessee for haircuts at the black-owned Transitions East Salon and to seek financial advice at a brokerage firm in that same city.

In the fall of 2004, I was asked to play for the wedding of Ann Hill, (the Emory & Henry board member who had been instrumental in my being hired by the college—see chapter 7). Ann's wedding was held in the college's chapel. This event was only the first of a series of musical performances on campus. In all of my years of living in Richmond, few people knew of my musical abilities; rarely did I play the piano. (There were very few musical events at JSRCC!) In 1976, I did travel to Roanoke to play for the wedding of Paul Montgomery, a one-time member of the Ebenezer Church Junior Choir. There was an Abingdon wedding in 2005 (David Lee) and another Emory and Henry wedding in 2006 (Dennis Hill Jr.). I really enjoyed all of these musical performances!

In my early days of teaching at Emory & Henry College, I realized some of the significant differences in teaching in a church-affiliated, private school versus teaching in a state-supported school. For example, commencement exercises at JSRCC had no religious overtones—no singing, invocations, or benedictions. Because of my religious background, I felt somewhat empty with respect to these "politically correct" celebrations. At an EHC event in my first week on campus, I was visibly moved when the concert choir performed "The Lord Bless You and Keep You." My mind suddenly went back to my days at Bristol's Douglass High School; our glee club often sang this awe-inspiring song. I try *not* to get too emotional at the sound of a musical performance. But sometimes a stoic persona is not possible!

Beginning in 2004, I started playing piano at Charles Wesley United Methodist Church in Abingdon when the pianist there became ill. I played at this church on those Sundays when I did not play at my Glade Spring church. Charles Wesley had a men's choir that was well known around the area. I became excited to become involved with this musical group—music had been a positive emotional outlet for me for decades. In the first few years at Charles Wesley (one of only three black Methodist churches in Holston's Abingdon District), we performed at a number of churches. There are pros and cons when it comes to playing by ear. Reading the music (on sight) is difficult, at best. However, once a song is learned, it is often possible to play in a key that is suitable for the singers. By playing for the Charles Wesley Men's Choir, I realized that many songs were written in keys that were way too high for some voices. Being able to pick a key that is suitable is something that I consider to be an advantage.

David Montgomery, a Plum Creek native, was attending Ebenezer Church at this time; he decided to join me when I performed at Charles Wesley Church. Although David had been singing in the Glade Spring area for a number of years, he seemed to reach a new level of excellence beginning in 2004. He visited Emory & Henry often and became intrigued by the college's music department. He was asked to sing "O Holy Night" at an Emory & Henry Christmas service. Excitedly, he commented that it was his first time singing in the chapel and that it was something he always wanted to do. There were times when David performed small jobs for me—preparing diskettes that I needed for the EHC administration of the Tek.Xam, a computer proficiency exam.

One of the down-sides to being known for piano playing in the region was the number of funerals in which I became involved. At one point, I realized that I'd attended close to thirty funerals since returning home. Although I did not play for all of them, for many of them I did. Aside from family members, there were the deaths of church members, old friends and schoolmates, and members of the Emory & Henry College community.

When my mother died in March 2005, one of my concerns was that I did not have an extended family from which I could draw support. My cousin Dyann and her husband, Robert, were able to drive in from Maryland. I also had the support of Abingdon cousins Ann Newton and Ellen Carter, as well as Aunt Ethel Smith. David Montgomery and the Tolliver family were also supportive. Unexpectedly, the support of the Emory & Henry College community was equally amazing. Several members, including the dean of faculty and the president's wife, attended the funeral; countless others expressed their sympathy in a variety of ways. Anita Coulthard, the college's organist, Tim Kobler, the college's chaplain, and student preacher Nathan Kilbourne played key roles in the service. Students acted as pallbearers, and former Ebenezer Church pastor, Rev. Dr. William Weldon, delivered the eulogy.

As mentioned in earlier chapters, my involvement in Ebenezer United Methodist Church has been significant for many decades. This has definitely been the case since returning home in 2001. In the early years, I produced Sunday afternoon singing events as often as twice a year. One event was usually in the spring, and the other was usually in the fall. I had scheduled one of these events for the first Sunday in April 2005. This service was scheduled the day before my mother's funeral; I chose not to cancel. Instead, I conducted the singing and used it as a tribute to her lifetime of service to the church. There have been so many things in my life that have happened largely beyond the realm of my control.

After my mother's death, I returned to my job at Emory & Henry, thankfully having somewhere to go regularly to ease my transition into what could be considered a new phase of my life.

Only a few weeks after my mother was buried, I was at home alone one day, writing thank-you notes to all of the people who had been so kind during my time of bereavement. An incident occurred that required that I call the Town of Glade Spring and ask for a policeman to come to my house. Not wishing to give too many details about this incident, I feel it is important that I comment about the demeanor of the policeman who came to my house. With no provocation, this veteran policeman went off on me, standing on my front porch and using profanity that was worse than anything I had ever heard in Baltimore, Richmond, or anywhere I had lived before. I was in a state of shock! After gaining my composure, I immediately called longtime friend Marie Brown, who was then a member of the Glade Spring Town Council. I told her what had happened. Although I am considered by most people to be a mild-mannered individual, I indicated to the town authorities that if this policeman was not fired, I was going to sue. He was gone the next day! This same policeman had visited my home once before—the night in 2003 when a vacant house was set afire on my street. I attributed his accusatory tone that night to the excitement of the moment. A related event was the refusal of the town's sanitation department to pick up my garbage on the day after the incident with the policeman. I told the mayor that if my garbage was not picked up (a service for which I had paid), I was going to bring the trash to the town hall and dump it on the front steps. The pickup occurred immediately! Mild-mannered people do have a breaking point!

The incidents described above were indicative of a town government that had reached a low point. As minority residents of Glade Spring, my mother and grandmother had problems with the town over the decades. Since I was going to apparently spend the rest of my life in Glade Spring, I began to think how I could make certain that fairness for all citizens was the rule rather than the exception! Perhaps it was at this point that I thought about getting involved in community service.

Over the next several months, I became more and more involved in community events—church services, civic club meetings, and countless events associated with Emory

& Henry College. Always on the shy side, I found myself continually involved in activities that were beyond my usual comfort zone. I decided to enroll in special training so that I could become a certified lay speaker in the Methodist Church. Additionally, I organized Black History events at the college, performed solos and led songs at various churches, and accepted invitations to speak at many area churches. It had not been my original intent to lead a high-profile life in the area. Many of these activities seemed to occur by default. Someone was needed; here I was!

By early 2006, I had made a decision to run for a seat on the Glade Spring Town Council. In retrospect, if I had analyzed the situation more carefully, I probably would *not* have considered transitioning into the realm of local politics. Historically, most people who run for local office have a business, civic, and/or entrepreneurial background. Rarely is the background for local elected officeholders that of education—especially educators at the college level. Nevertheless, I completed the necessary paperwork in February of 2006, the first individual to do so. Immediately, several individuals came forward and offered help in the campaign. Jim Bradley and David Montgomery were longtime friends who assisted in a variety of ways. Financial support came from a variety of sources, including members of an Abingdon law firm. Additionally, Dirk Moore (the EHC director of public relations) and Diane Johnson of the Glade Civic Club provided support. Signs were printed and placed in yards throughout the town. A large banner was placed in my own yard. Ironically, this banner was stolen early on Easter Sunday morning. In my mind, the symbolism of this theft was highly significant.

Three slots on the town council were to be filled as a result of the election of May 2006. Seven people ran for those slots—newcomers and incumbents. A debate was co-sponsored by the local chapter of the League of Women Voters and the Glade Spring Civic Club. A few candidates did not participate in this debate. For whatever reason, my composure during this event was apparent. My humor again came to the forefront! In retrospect, I am convinced that not taking myself too seriously is an incalculable asset.

Election Day of 2006 was surreal. I did not anticipate the outcome. Plans had been made for people to gather at my house when the results were announced. We candidates stayed at the town hall to wait for voting officials to complete their tallies. The discovery that I was the top vote-getter was a fact that was difficult for me to process. Many of the other candidates were highly qualified with the requisite backgrounds mentioned earlier. It was my personal belief that many voters remembered my mother and concluded that my integrity was comparable to hers! When I arrived at my home, the yard was full of cars. The election-night celebration was very memorable. Briefly, I thought about what my mother's reaction would have been. Knowing how excited she was when people visited her home, I was convinced that she would have readily and happily greeted all of the celebrants!

Even before our tenure as new town council members officially began, there were several preliminary meetings that we attended. One such meeting was held at Abingdon's Martha Washington Inn. This was the first time that I had ever been in this historic building—a building famous throughout the region and beyond. Of course, I would not have been allowed in this building (unless working there) in my formative years in the area. Three years later, in my role as professor at Emory and Henry College, I attended a meeting at Marion's Hungry Mother State Park. This was my first time in this facility. Blacks were similarly prevented from being there in earlier years. These two events, personally speaking, were representative of the title of this book: *Go and Come Again*!

The start of my four-year tenure on the Glade Spring Town Council coincided with an increase in responsibilities at Emory & Henry College. In the early years at the school, my primary focus was the teaching of the various computer classes. By 2007, however, I was becoming more involved in faculty advising, curriculum development, and special activities and events, such as the 2008 Virginia Highlands Festival Lecture and Concert. There were times that I felt that I should give up my Town Council position. There were just not enough hours in the day to get things done. Additionally, there were the ever-present responsibilities associated with the musical, administrative, and custodial tasks at Ebenezer United Methodist Church. However, I did my best to meet all of these responsibilities. In four years on the council, I never missed a single regularly scheduled monthly meeting. Moreover, I never missed an EHC faculty meeting in a seven-year period.

In August of 2007, an incident occurred that may have been related to my high profile status in my hometown. Not considered to be a trailblazer on the town council, however, it is hard for me to imagine how anyone in the community could have considered me a threat. Nevertheless, the incident happened. My vehicles were vandalized while parked under a streetlight beside my home, and with me sleeping only a few feet away. It is my strong belief that, for some reason, I was singled out. Other parked cars on the street were not touched. More than $1000 in damage occurred! The perpetrator(s) were never caught. I'd never experienced vandalism in the twenty-seven years that I lived in Richmond. The fact that something like this happened in the town where I was born and reared was difficult for me to comprehend. Of course, times are different. As a child growing up in the 1950s, rarely did we lock our doors. Some doors could not be locked! Now, being on guard is an ever-present prospect!

One of my mother's old sayings was: "Turn a lemon into lemonade." Essentially, this means turning a bad situation into something good. This is what I decided to do. By early

2008, I started on a major renovation to my historic home—a breezeway, sunroom, and two-vehicle garage additions. This project was completed over an extended period of about one year. If the vehicles had never been vandalized, I probably would have never invested in such a construction venture—a venture that revolutionized the appearance of my home and the neighborhood.

Only a few months have passed since finishing my term on the Glade Spring Town Council; therefore, I have difficulty in assessing the totality of the experience. There were some occasions when I was the only person to vote against a particular issue. Surprisingly, I often felt a sense of pride in standing up for something in which I believed. It is usually much easier to follow the crowd. One project of which I was totally supportive was the renovation of the former Peery grocery store as the new location for the town's library. In my first year in office, I donated $1000 to the library fund drive—a donation that was given in memory of my mother. As the new library opened in 2011, I pledged additional funds.

While serving on the Glade Spring Town Council, I was the only African-American member. However, I was not the first black to serve; I was the fifth. I always thought this was a positive reflection on our town inasmuch as many other towns in the area never had a black person to be elected to any office. The black population of Glade Spring is comparatively low (a percentage in the single digits). While on the council, I was most likely the only black officeholder in the immediate area.

While being an elected official, only once was race interjected as a would-be issue. This particular issue, although never discussed by the council while I was a member, originated when a new citizen vaguely alleged that I was discriminating against him because he was *white*—an issue which was resoundingly dismissed as being without merit. A close friend jokingly called me Jerry-Jones-*Comma*-Black—a reference to the *insulting* manner in which I was identified in this so-called written complaint! I can think of so many other words that could have more fittingly followed the comma—referring to the phrase in Dr. Martin Luther King's speech which noted that people should be judged by the content of their character rather than the color of their skin!

My associations at Emory & Henry College have been great. I have learned so many things from faculty, staff, and students. For example, many faculty members and students have traveled extensively. Although older than many of my EHC colleagues, my travel experiences were primarily nonexistent! Except for computer educator conferences and visits to family members, I did not travel. A year or two after my mother's death, largely at the suggestion of cousins and close friends, I decided to spend some time traveling—especially during the summer months. To commemorate my sixtieth birthday in 2007, I decided to expand my horizons. I went on a transatlantic cruise—sailing from New York to London on the Queen Mary 2 cruise liner. This was my first time out of the country! Subsequent trips have taken me to France, Germany, the Caribbean, and the Baltic region of Europe. Such journeys would have been unimaginable a few years ago. The experiences have been totally rewarding—meeting interesting people, seeing countless sights, and learning about different cultures, languages, and religions. I hope to continue these explorations! In 2007, it was also my honor to host a faculty social in my historic Glade Spring home.

Maintaining a home is never easy—especially when the work is done by one individual. Additionally, when said house is more than 140 years old, the challenges are far greater. One of the unique features of the Johnston-Waugh-Jones house, aside from its age, is its location and the way in which it was torn apart in the early part of the twentieth century. In 1922, when a street was built in front of the house, the Town of Glade Spring decided that the structure would be too close to the pavement. Two rooms were disconnected, moved, and then hitched on to the back. Over the years, a number of problems surfaced that could be traced back to this rearrangement of the structure—doors that used to be windows, windows that used to be doors, and roofing slopes that were haphazardly joined together. At one point, the house had two front doors, only a few feet apart. There was no symmetry to the main portion of the structure (unlike the original pre-1922 design), cracks were everywhere, and the foundation was very unstable.

In 1972, the entire ground floor of our home was flooded—an incident that was caused primarily by discarded trash upstream and fill-ins downstream. My mother had to escape the house in the middle of the night—not knowing if the house would be completely under water.

Over 140 years, neighbors have come and gone. When I was a child in the 1950s, about ten homes were on our street—inhabited by both black and white people. My fondest memories of past neighbors include names like Porter, Sandefur, Jollie, Price, Stuart, Skipper, White, Brewster, Thomas, Ballou, Edwards, and Rhudy. All of these homes, facing the railroad, were on a thoroughfare that was essentially the main street leading into the town square from the east. Today, only a few houses remain!

Over the years, many contractors have worked on the Johnston-Waugh-Jones house. In my early years, I witnessed a number of people trying to take advantage of my mother in regard to fixing the house. The fact that she was female, black, and single played into the mind-set of some individuals. As I got older, I instinctively knew what was workable and what should be done. As a teenager, I often talked with Mom privately and told her my concerns about the work being done on our home. She would then tell the workers how she wanted the job to be completed. In later years, there have been some contractors who *tried* to take advantage of me. Some things seem to never change!

Over a period of more than forty years, Mom and I worked as a team with respect to keeping the old house standing. Now that I am the sole owner and occupant, I am thankful that we put forth the earlier efforts. At least, I have a fairly decent place in which to live after spending so many years in places like Richmond and Baltimore.

Two adjoining properties on my street now belong to me—one purchased in 1982 and the other purchased in 2004. Now the old house sits on about a three-fourth-acre lot—bordered on the south by crape myrtles and other blooming bushes. Yard work, time consuming and sometimes difficult, has always provided me with pleasure, exercise, and a sense of pride. I continue to do my best in keeping the house and grounds in good shape.

In the summer of 2010, I should have been writing chapters of this book, but I could not resist being outside and doing yard work. I also could not resist doing inside jobs like wallpapering and painting. Even at my age, there are times when self-discipline is replaced by enjoyment!

Telling a story is not easy. There is always the feeling that something important may be left out or that something included should be rewritten or perhaps deleted. On the positive side, for a project that has been months in the making, it is rewarding to recall all of the encouragement received from friends, family, colleagues, and new acquaintances. Moreover, special thanks must be given to all who contributed facts, offered suggestions, and gave critical analyses.

Mary Waugh Jones, 1980s.

Robert "Bobby" Jones, 1950s.

Johnston-Waugh home, 1905.

Johnston-Waugh-Jones home, 2008.

The author's first "real" vacation—Queen Mary 2 cruise ship, 2007.

The author's vacation, northern (Baltic) Europe, 2010.

The author's vacation, northern (Baltic) Europe, 2010.

CHAPTER 10:
Predicting Academic Success

WHEN I WAS working on my doctoral degree at Virginia Polytechnic Institute and State University (Virginia Tech) in the 1970s, my dissertation was entitled "An Analysis of Selected Variables Relating to Levels of Academic Performance of First-Year Computer Programming Students in Virginia Community Colleges." In the review of literature of that research project of more than thirty years ago, the consequences of student failures were analyzed. Specifically, failures paralyze effort, keep aspirations low, and lower self-concept. A chapter summarization included the following concerns:

- Academically unsuccessful students *may* be weak in cognitive, abstract styles of learning.

- Academically unsuccessful students *may* possess one or more of the following characteristics: substandard language development, inferior auditory and visual discrimination, slow reading rates and poor reading comprehension, little or no motivation, and negative self-image.

- Past failures cloud the prospects of future success.

- Academically unsuccessful students *may* come from educationally, nutritionally, culturally, economically, physically, and/or motivationally poor family environments.

If one were to read the many stories of the academic success of so many black students in early-twentieth-century Southwest Virginia, a preliminary explanation of such success is not easy to quantify. Facilities were often poor or nonexistent, some teachers had less than a bachelor's degree, books and supplies were limited, and funding from local school systems was minimal. As mentioned in chapter 2, career teacher Harriet DeBose indicated that students "seemed to have come out pretty good; students ultimately became colonels in the army, doctors, lawyers, and teachers."

I would suspect that motivation, family support, and a sense of community might have something to do with the success of these educational pioneers, as well as hard work and having no sense of entitlement—not expecting things to be handed to you, expecting the government to provide for all aspects of life. Additionally, there were strong elements of discipline in the home, in the schools, in the churches, and in the communities.

For decades, educational experts have enumerated reasons why students do not succeed academically. As early as the 1960s, Sparks indicated that academically unsuccessful students come from families with characteristics like the following:

- Semiskilled or unskilled family heads
- Insufficient income to accommodate a reasonable level of living
- Substandard housing
- Inability to become a part of the majority culture
- Isolation from educational employment opportunities
- Disrupted and broken homes
- Dependency on service agencies for basic needs[1]

In the 1970s, experts indicated that the home environment can raise or curtail the individual's ability to achieve success in the classroom.

- The language of students from disadvantaged homes may be different from that used in school.

---

[1] Sparks, Mavis (1967). *Opportunities for the Disadvantaged in Office Education*. American Vocational Journal, 30.

- There may be inadequacies, such as inferior auditory and visual discrimination, poor judgment concerning time, and substandard number skills.

- Manifestations associated with a negative self-image include extremely high or extremely low levels of aspiration, fear of failure, low academic motivation, and withdrawal.

- The motivation of the academically unsuccessful student is not usually internal.[2]

Tonne and Nanassy, authorities in the area of business and technical education, provided an additional definition to the term "academically unsuccessful student" in the 1970s:

> Cultural deprivation usually results in having little motivation. [These students] are characterized by poor work habits, poor attitudes, frequent absences from school, inferiority complex, inability to work independently, and short interest and attention span.[3]

According to Scott, millions of American citizens are deficient in reading. Reasons for slow reading rates and poor comprehension include the following:

- Lack of background experiences and limited vocabulary.
- Conscious or unconscious moving of the lips
- Reading every piece of material at the same rate
- Lack of concentration on reading materials.[4]

Writing in 2004, Claude Steele, associated with the Department of Psychology at Stanford University, wrote about stereotype threat:

---

[2] Bailey, Larry and Stadt, Ronald (1973). *Career Education*. McKnight Publishers.

[3] Tonne, Herbert and Nanassy, Louis (1970). *Principles of Business Education*. McGraw-Hill Publishers, *131-133*.

[4] Scott, James. (1974) *Business Education Forum, 31-32*.

> [Some studies dealt with] the academic underperformance of groups whose abilities are negatively stereotyped. The underperformance of such groups...can stem in significant part from stereotype threat, the threat of confirming or being seen to confirm negative stereotypes about their group's abilities in critical performance situations. [5]

Also writing in 2004, Sandra Graham, associated with the Department of Education, University of California, Los Angeles, examined motivation as it relates to black students:

> [It] might be argued that many Black students do poorly in school because their own life experiences are discrepant with the notion that students ought to feel morally obligated to exert effort in school. For example, I hear comments such as 'They can do the work but they just don't seem to care' or 'The kids have not come to terms with the reality that you have to work hard in school to guarantee success in life.'[6]

Self-analysis can be a dangerous thing! However, based on a review of both past and present literature, I perhaps should *not* have been very academically successful. Consider the following socioeconomic factors:

- I was raised by a single mother who struggled financially.
- My mother was not a college graduate.
- Our home had no indoor bathroom in the 1950s.
- Our home was not centrally heated.
- Our home was often in need of repair.
- There were limited learning resources in the home.

---

[5] Philogène, Gina (Editor) (2004). *Racial Identity in Context.* American Psychological Association, Washington DC, 66-67.

[6] Philogène, Gina (Editor) (2004). *Racial Identity in Context.* American Psychological Association, Washington DC, 126-127.

- We never owned an automobile; travel was limited.
- We were on welfare in the early 1950s.

There were a number of cultural circumstances that could have also made my academic success unlikely.

- After-school activities were limited.
- Black churches had no outreach programs.
- Black ministers did not live in our town.
- There were few local black professional role models.
- Few people in my community had college degrees.
- No one in my *immediate* family had attended college.
- Kindergarten, Head Start, preschool, and scouting were unavailable. Our high school was nearly thirty miles from home.
- Our town did not have a library.

In retrospect, there were some personal attributes that could have impacted on my academic success.

- I was extremely shy and underweight.
- I was not athletically inclined.
- I was not very healthy during childhood.
- I was the only left-handed student in the entire elementary school.
- My only sibling was almost twelve years older.

Finally, there were the political circumstances of the American South in the 1950s and the early 1960s—circumstances that play into the notion of "stereotype threat," that a black student is somehow genetically less able to succeed academically.

- Public accommodations were segregated.
- Our public schools were "separate and unequal."
- Racial slurs were sometimes heard.

With respect to the notion that somehow I was continually being reminded that my academic success was unlikely, I do not recall hearing any such comments. No one—friends or family, teachers, or white neighbors—ever said anything to me that made me think that I was not going to be successful. The contrary was universally heard. "Keep studying and working hard, and you will be fine." Furthermore, I do not recall statements in the media—radio, television, or newspapers—that made any suggestions that black students were somehow less able to learn. In fact, I don't recall hearing much about black people at all until the civil rights efforts became more pronounced in the early 1960s. And even then, my surrounding region did not witness the hostility and violence that other areas experienced as integration started to have momentum.

Regarding some of my personal attributes—being left-handed, underweight, and shy—these matters became less and less an issue as I started to excel in the early elementary grades. My home economic situation was about the same as that of everyone else with whom I went to school and played. My neighborhood, racially integrated from my earliest recollections, encompassed households that, for the most part, were at the same economic level.

Because of the support and encouragement of my teachers, my motivation became more and more internal. With respect to my reading rate, I recall Mr. Anderson stating (at about grade six) that my reading rate was somewhat slow. He provided me with some exercises that allowed this rate to increase.

With respect to hearing racial slurs, such events were few and far between. In my view, these incidents were not internalized and had no effect on self-image or self-esteem. If anything, it made all of us determined to excel even more in school, knowing that eventually we would have a better life. We would overcome!

In my opinion, the primary reasons for my success in school can be summarized as follows:

- My mother always helped me with homework, visited the schools often, participated in PTA, conferred with teachers on a regular basis, and was the ultimate role model with respect to hard work.

- My teachers were always supportive and were excellent role models; they visited my home.

- The successes of my mother's family—brothers and sister—provided excellent role models.

- The success of my brother in the military provided an excellent role model.

- Community and church elders networked to ensure that we children were always behaving as we should.

- My verbal skills were improved by listening to a variety of programming on the radio. Some of these programs included *Paul Harvey News and Comment*, Don McNeill's *The Breakfast Club*, and fifteen-minute soap operas!

- During the golden age of television, there were countless programs that taught morality and life lessons. Some of these programs included *Captain Kangaroo, Sky King, Roy Rogers, The Lone Ranger, What's My Line*, newscasts, and sports events. Variety programming like *The Ed Sullivan Show* expanded cultural knowledge, showcased role models, and provided amazing entertainment.

- My mother encouraged me to read newspapers and magazines, such as *Ebony* and *Jet*.

- Sunday school, the church, and vacation Bible school provided additional learning opportunities.

- Community and church events, such as picnics and church dinners, continually reinforced the sense of community and the feeling that my small family was a part of a larger social dynamic.

- Playtime was varied, physically and mentally stimulating, and entertaining.

- Playmates were racially diverse, interesting, and levelheaded; many became lifelong friends.

- There were opportunities to learn economic responsibility—selling cards, candy, mottos, and other items.

- Part-time jobs were ongoing.

- Helping with home maintenance and repairs was encouraged.

- Learning to play the piano improved my mind, mitigated shyness, advanced self-esteem, and provided enjoyment.

The sense of humor that surrounded me in childhood—from family, friends, and neighbors—became a part of my own personality. I never took myself very seriously! This trait has served me well in all academic pursuits and career levels.

Our home was constantly visited by family from far and near, and everyone had a story to tell. I listened very intently! Furthermore, our home was also visited by friends, neighbors, travelers, salesmen, people performing repairs, and vendors delivering goods and services. They also had stories to tell. Melinda Blau and Karen Fingerman, writing in 2009, referred to these people as "consequential strangers":

> Every day we interact with people who influence our lives in a small and great ways but who are not part of our inner circle. Each of these relations is different from the other, but they all are consequential strangers—people who are so much a part of our everyday life that we often take them for granted. [They] anchor us in the world and give us a sense of being plugged into something larger. They also enhance and enrich our lives and offer us opportunities for novel experiences and information that is beyond the purview of our inner circles.[7]

In looking back on my childhood, I am amazed how freely people discussed such a wide variety of topics in our home. My conclusion is that my mother's personality was such that everyone felt so welcome and free to share their thoughts. For this enriching environment, I am truly grateful!

---

[7] Blau, Melinda and Fingerman, Karen (2009). *Consequential Strangers*. W. W. Norton & Company, New York, xvi.

Glade Spring's "colored" elementary school (a Rosenwald Foundation school).

The author heading to school in 1953.

Second grade, Glade Spring's "colored" elementary school, 1954.
(Left to right) Jerry Jones, Leona Hayes, Nina Porter, Margaret Porter, Kyle Bradley, and Paul Ervin.

Croquet players in the Joneses' yard, late 1950s.
(Left to right) Kyle Bradley, Jimmy Bradley, Frankie Skipper, David Bradley, and Jerry Jones.

The author on his bike in the Joneses' back yard, early 1960s.

The author at his piano, early 1960s.

Conclusion

AS OUTLINED IN earlier chapters of this book, many black people left Southwest Virginia to escape segregation, racism, and the Jim Crow mind-set of the latter portion of the nineteenth century and much of the twentieth century. It was necessary to leave for educational pursuits and jobs. Recently, statistical experts have indicated that many minority citizens are returning to the South—especially to urban centers like Atlanta, Georgia, and Charlotte, North Carolina. Stated reasons for these relocations include economic opportunities as well as the desire to reconnect with ancestral roots. There are those who say that in some respects the opportunities in the Sun Belt are actually better than those found in many northern areas.

I am sure that some sections of Virginia will see the return of many black people. There are indications that the Northern Virginia suburbs near Washington DC are approaching a "majority minority" status. Whether this status will occur in other areas of the state is difficult to predict.

Over the past five decades, I have witnessed the black population of Southwest Virginia decline dramatically. Additionally, I have seen very few natives of other races returning to this area. Of course, certain counties have more diverse populations than others.

As a child in the 1950s and early 1960s, I rarely thought about the strength and vibrant nature of the African-American population of my hometown. As I became involved in the writing of this book, however, I realized that there was a minority presence that was worthy of notice, respect, and admiration. There were black business owners and other professionals. In certain chapters, for example, references were made to the many Glade Spring black-owned restaurants in the first half of the twentieth century—Savage, Davis, Skipper, and Stuart. Moreover, there were shoe shops (Hounshell and Coleman) as well as Wiley Waugh's barber shop and the Brise cleaning and pressing shop.

Except for the Tri-Cities (Bristol, Kingsport, and Johnson City), today there are only a few blacks in the entire region. As a result, many historically-black churches have closed. Some remaining churches have dangerously-low memberships. Fortunately, some churches, including Ebenezer United Methodist in Glade Spring, have realized that they must have a more integrated profile in order to survive!

A positive observation is that exclusively black neighborhoods, especially in the small towns of Southwest Virginia, are increasingly rare. There may be only a few blacks, but they tend to live in geographically-dispersed areas and usually have white neighbors.

If one is to accept the premise that blacks are leaving certain northern urban areas and relocating to the South, then one must enumerate the probable reasons. The comments often heard include the following: less hectic life, less noise, lower probability of terrorist activities and other crimes, warmer climate, and a lower cost of living.

When the school systems of my native area were integrated in the mid-1960s, many black school teachers had to leave the area to seek employment. Only a handful of black teachers were employed in the integrated systems. Georgia Polk, a Glade Spring native, and Harriet DeBose, an Abingdon native, both were area educators for more than forty years. Today, in some Southwest Virginia school districts, it is possible that a white student never has a black classmate or a black teacher. Even at the college level, a black professor is rare at best. As the date of my retirement from Emory & Henry approaches, I would love to see a minority presence on this faculty.

If I had an opportunity to talk with black families from across the United States, I would eagerly present the case that they should consider relocating to Southwest Virginia. As a teacher who has worked in high schools, community colleges, and four-year colleges, I can state unequivocally that education in the area is superior. Additionally, there is a friendly nature and calmness encountered in the area, the economy is diverse, the climate is moderate, interstate highways are toll-free, and the scenery in breathtaking.

Often people hear the stereotypes that residents of the area known as Appalachia are educationally, religiously, politically, culturally, and economically homogeneous. I find this to be totally untrue! Whatever one's beliefs, persuasions, and life circumstances, this area is welcoming to all!

CPSIA information can be obtained at www.ICGtesting.com
Printed in the USA
BVOW042247260212

283794BV00005B/8/P